I Survived Suicide

by Killing Myself

From Pain to Purpose: This Isn't Just a Memoir—It's a
Daily Reminder That Who You Become Is Up to You, and
the Life You Deserve Is Yours to Create.

Trapper Searles

ISBN Paperback: 979-8-89576-116-8
ISBN Hardback: 979-8-89576-117-5

Published by:

This book is dedicated to those who have faced life's darkest valleys and dared to climb its highest peaks.

This book is for you -

For the dreamers, doers, and believers who see possibilities in impossibilities.

May this journey remind you that perspective is the most powerful tool we possess.

With gratitude, hope, and a relentless belief in brighter tomorrows, this book is dedicated to you.

Today is the best day of your life!

Table of Contents

Prologue

This Book Isn't Just My Story—It's Yours, Too.

I didn't set out to write a book. I set out to serve.

This book began as scribbled journal entries—fragments of pain, flashes of perspective, whispers of hope I wasn't even sure I believed yet. I wasn't trying to be profound. I was trying not to break.

But somewhere along the way, the words became more than therapy. They became truth. And that truth is this: the lowest moments of your life aren't rock bottom—they're the foundation for something greater.

This book is a memoir, yes. It holds the unfiltered story of my life—from a broken boy with buried trauma to a man who nearly lost everything, including himself.

But more importantly, this book is also a guide. A mirror. A challenge.

Because chances are, you're not just here to learn about *my* pain—you're here to heal your own. You're looking for clarity, connection, maybe even a lifeline.

So let me be clear: *I Survived Suicide by Killing Myself* isn't about glorifying the fall. It's about rewriting what comes after. It's a roadmap for rebuilding from the inside out—using perspective, energy, and truth as tools to rise from what nearly destroyed you.

You don't need perfect circumstances. You need an honest perspective and the willingness to step into the fire and come out forged.

If you've ever felt lost, numb, angry, ashamed, or like the person in the mirror is a stranger, you're not alone. And you're not broken.

Let's walk this road together.

You're still here. That means something.

Let's figure out what.

— Trapper

Introduction

My wife left me emotionally long before I was aware of it. It wasn't until 2015 that I discovered her connection with her first love—a boy she'd known in middle school. I found texts, emails, and expressions of love and intimacy that she and I hadn't shared for years.

My heart hurt. I loved Sam beyond reason. "What do I need to change?" I asked her. "What do I need to fix?"

We went to counseling. Her issues were completely justified. I wasn't supporting her emotionally, and I wasn't spending time with our family. I was obsessed with work because success meant money, didn't it?

Maybe I had to change my perspective. I enrolled in the *Tap Your Potential* program, led by Dr. Sabrina Starling. The essence of the program can best be expressed this way: "You're going to commit to doing what we tell you to do because we know that it will change your life."

I don't like being told what to do, so I entered the program kicking and screaming all the way. *You're telling me to change my business hours? What do you mean, I can't work weekends? I can't be on call 24/7?*

I fought it, but I also stuck with it because I loved Sam and my marriage mattered. Bit by bit, I began to make changes. When I saw their impact, I stopped fighting the process. I'd been an okay dad, but if you'd asked me where my daughter went to school, I wouldn't have been able to tell you. I became a good dad.

Sam and I continued to get counseling, and our marriage improved. I was more present with her. We were still struggling, but we were also doing better. Then, I found another text message from her old boyfriend.

My already low self-esteem plunged into an abyss. And then I felt a red-hot rage. I had done everything she'd asked me to. I had changed! Why wasn't that enough?

What reason did I have to keep going? My life was being stolen from me. Everything I wanted and everything I'd worked for – it was all meaningless. Sam and I had been married eleven years, and I loved her with all my heart. I had never wavered. But this marriage I treasured was fake. The happy couple everyone saw – it was all a lie.

She was in love with another man, and he'd been arrested for grand theft. My wife thought I was so awful, she wanted to be with an ex-con instead of a successful man doing everything in his power to look after his family. My self-esteem plunged even lower.

I took my misery and depression to Tamara, my therapist, who suggested I leave the marriage. But Sam had changed my life from the minute I met her. I could as easily stop loving her as I could cease breathing.

Months passed, and slowly we came back together. And then, after a beautiful night of real conversation and heartfelt intimacy, her phone pinged. On her Snapchat account were photos from the old boyfriend I never wanted to see.

A couple of days later, I read some entries in her diary. No, I shouldn't have done that, but I was beyond reason. I learned how very much she didn't like me and how she wished she had the courage to leave. That's when I knew for certain that she and our daughter, Jaiden, would be happier without me.

Not long after that, I went on a fishing trip with my buddies up in the mountains. I'd always been afraid of heights and depths, but on the river was an area with deep water where people cliff-jumped. I climbed to the top of the cliff because dying in the river couldn't be any worse than what I had planned.

I jumped, eyes closed, and hit the water. No sound – was I down there a lifetime or only a few seconds? Time had stopped following manmade rules. I was alone and at peace in a place no one could see or hear me.

Later that night, after dinner around the campfire, I told my friends I was going to drive to the top of the mountain where I would have enough reception to call Jaiden. I drove up in my big F450, high above the valley floor, where Jaiden and I chatted like it was just another normal day.

"I love you so much," I said as I ended the call.

"Do you want to talk to Mom?"

"No. I love you."

I ended the call and sat behind the wheel, looking down the long straightaway before the first switchback turn of the road. A sense of calm floated down over me like a soft cloud. I knew Sam and Jaiden would be okay. I knew Sam wanted me gone, and that she'd be happier with her old boyfriend. I could do this for her – a last act of devotion. I also had a great insurance policy, and a truck going over a cliff would look like an accident. Probably I'd fallen asleep at the wheel.

My thoughts fell away. With peace and a clear purpose, I pressed down on the gas. The big truck picked up speed: 100, 110, 120, 140. Then my dash lit up: a call from Stinkybean, my pet name for Jaiden. I was about 150 feet from the guardrail. But my daughter needed me.

I hit the brakes and came to a stop short of the guardrail.

"Hey, Stink! What's up?"

"Hey, Dad. You didn't sound good earlier. Can you come home tonight?"

"Yeah."

I drove to the bottom of the mountain, said goodbye to my friends, and drove the four hours home to Denver.

If this had been a movie, Sam would have wept and greeted me at home with open arms and a promise that things would be different. But real life isn't a Hollywood script. Sam didn't cry, and she didn't have to. Everything began to change for me when Jaiden called and asked me to come home. That's when I knew I had a purpose. I recognized I was loved.

Seconds before that call, when I knew I was about to die, I'd let go of who I was.

Maybe my body didn't die, but that particular me did. On the drive home, I was a reborn man. I had a new opportunity—a chance to let go of the past me and be who I wanted to be. Most importantly, I had the opportunity to learn how to love myself.

I could begin to ask, "Who am I?" and genuinely discover the answer. I had never given myself the time to look deep inside. I'd been wrapped up in work and building the material trappings of success. I'd had to take care of others. Now, it was time to take care of myself, and that was the beginning of another revelation: if I didn't take care of myself, how could I adequately take care of others? If I wasn't whole and healthy, how could I give the best of myself to those I loved?

I've told people that I survived suicide.

But I didn't.

I died and I was reborn.

But here's what I believe: you don't have to attempt suicide to be reborn and to discover who you truly are. You can make a choice to change and become authentic, vulnerable, and real. The pain you feel is the pain of not being you.

You can look inside and understand who you want to be, not who others want you to be. Many people, and society at large, place expectations on us, and we can easily fall into the trap of trying to live up to those expectations for our entire lives. I don't want to be someone for the sake of another. I want to be someone for myself. I believe everyone wants and deserves that.

I want to make myself proud. I want my daughter to be proud of who I am, and I want her to be proud of herself. If you're reading this, I want you to be able to say "Fuck everyone else. I just want to be the best me."

If you can be genuinely you, it serves everyone you love and care about. I'd been trying to serve Sam by striving to be what she wanted me to be. Our relationship is stronger today because I gave up on that - I killed that old me and became my authentic self.

I lived my whole life being whoever others wanted me to be. When I was growing up, I did what most kids do—I became the person my parents told me to be. In the family I grew up in, that wasn't a winning strategy.

CHAPTER 1

Childhood

I grew up in a dysfunctional family.

I didn't know that when I was a little kid, but it was pretty bad. My childhood home is engraved in my mind. It was a small, 3-bedroom, 1-bathroom house backed up to train tracks, then a highway. I was born February 16, 1983, in Casper, Wyoming. I'm sure the wind was howling and the snow was several feet deep when my parents brought me home from the local hospital. I'm not sure who welcomed me to our little 3-bedroom house, but it was a crowded one. We lived with my Uncle Bob, Aunt Jeanette, my older sister, Amber, and Grandma Gloria. Did they pass me around for cuddles? Did they take a look and shrug? Did they worry because one more human being would stretch scarce resources even thinner?

One thing I'm sure about: my grandmother Gloria would have fallen in love with me at first sight, and I suspect the feeling was entirely mutual. Gloria was my mother's mother, whose husband died when her youngest son, my Uncle Bob, was only a year old. She was consequently declared mentally unstable by the state, incapable of looking after her children. Because my mother was an adult and desperate to keep the family together, she took in her mother and her younger siblings.

Grandma Gloria was the most amazing woman I have ever met. I knew she was awesome, even when I was young, but it took years for the full extent of her magnificence to sink in. She smoked at least three packs of Camels a day, collecting *Camel bucks* and using them to buy us presents at Christmas and on our birthdays. I had a fabulous new winter coat one year with Joe Camel stamped on the back, a cigarette dangling saucily from his mouth. She was probably as crazy as diagnosed, but in a good way. She refused to take her meds, and it didn't matter because she was as sweet as an angel. Where my parents were rushing river rapids with dangerous boulders just under the surface, she was a deep, still pool, shining in the sun.

She would tickle and scratch our backs with her impossibly long fingernails, and play itsy bitsy spider up our spines, and then the spider fell down - and then - and then it was pure, original Gloria: "And then he got shot!" And bang, she'd hit your backbone with a pointed finger.

"Ow!"

But we kept coming back for more.

My mom and dad shared a bedroom. The rest of us crammed into the space that was left, with Uncle Jim in and out almost every day. I remember "rooming" in our unfinished basement for a while. One night, I dreamed about a spider slowly weaving its way down to my face. I woke up and turned on my lamp, and there it was —a giant black widow spider!

Clap! Dead spider! I'm pretty sure I didn't sleep much the rest of that night. In fact, I probably climbed the stairs to my sister Amber's room, lying down on the floor at the end of her bed. I spent quite a few nights there.

I was told that my dad was an alcoholic. That's not how I remember him. The version I saw was abusive to my mother, loud, angry, and at least once, startlingly insightful. The fights my parents had were often epic. On one occasion, he nearly tossed her through the living room window. When the police would arrive, they would take him into custody, and off he went. It wasn't the first time he spent a night at the detention center.

My mother wasn't innocent in this. She knew his buttons and pushed them with pinpoint precision, watching for his reactions. The more agitated he became, the more accurately she aimed her barbs. She didn't trust him. She suspected he'd had an affair at some point. He was no good. She knew how the fight would end, but she was a runaway train with failed brakes. When he erupted, the entire house became a battle zone. Whatever they could grab, they hurled across the room, their voices ricocheting off the walls.

My Aunt Jeannette and my sister Amber protected me from the worst of it. They knew the signs of impending war, and would take me for a walk, or Amber would bring me into her room. If we hadn't escaped in time, we would become my mother's weapons. "I'm going to leave and take the kids," or, "Get out of here - leave me and the kids."

I loved my mom, and if there were sides to take in the battles, I took hers. How could I not? Dad hurt her, didn't he? But maybe that was normal, and this was just what growing up in a family looked like: fights, yelling, hitting, walking away, police, and then, a few times a year, family trips that were as close to heaven as it could possibly get.

We had a ratty old camper that Dad would hook up to his Ramcharger; we'd pile in and drive to the Big Horn Mountains - just Mom, Dad, Amber, and me. We'd laugh and talk and play outside and sit around a campfire, huddled close to its warmth. My dad was right there, and my mom could let go of her suspicions.

I'm sure they loved each other with giant devotion, but their demons turned that love into fiery fear and hate far too often.

I had some good times with my dad, tagging along with him, Uncle Bob, and Uncle Jim when they went hunting for antelope. Then I was just like every other kid who went out with his dad during the fall season in central Wyoming.

I was about seven when my father decided he needed to teach Uncle Bob a lesson, bringing me into it as well. Bob was treating Mom, his older sister, badly, and that wasn't okay with Dad. My mom was more than a sister to Bob; she'd raised him as well. Dad may have lashed out fiercely at my mother, but if one of us was disrespectful to her, we would answer to him. In his crazy way, he loved her beyond reason.

He grabbed Bob. "Get in the car. And, Trapper - you too. Get in the car."

Oh shit, I thought. *I didn't do anything.* But I didn't argue.

He drove his old two-toned brown Dodge Ramcharger to the Hat Six Ranch, where the owners had given him access for trapping and hunting. Dusk was turning to night as we drove up the dirt road, kicking up a plume of dust. There were no lights, no buildings - only prairie for as far as we could see. We bumped over a cattle guard and came to a stop at the side of the road, nosed into a small cottonwood.

"We're going to get out and go for a walk," Dad said to Uncle Bob. "Now, when you get out of the truck out here, you can scream and yell and cuss and swear and call Shellie anything you want to. You can do all that out here and get it out of your system. You just can't do it in front of her or in front of me."

We walked about two miles, crossing a cattle guard every few hundred yards, before Dad said we were going to turn around. "And I'm going to teach you guys a lesson. When you're pissed off, and you're frustrated, and you're angry, you step over things that can hurt you. You don't pay attention to your surroundings when you're pissed off. You say things you shouldn't say, and you don't understand the consequences of your words. We're going to walk back, and I'm going to show you something."

Dad used his flashlight to guide us back. The only other light was from a sliver of moon, and the sky was blanketed with stars. We crossed the first cattle guard. Dad aimed his flashlight down between the bars to reveal a rattlesnake den with maybe two hundred writhing critters.

My heart thumped so loudly I thought the snakes could probably hear it.

We crossed another cattle guard. Dad aimed his flashlight again. "Looks like a bunch more rattlesnakes."

We crossed four or five cattle guards, and it was rattlers all the way.

"You may be in a fit of rage somewhere," Dad said after the last crossing. "You may be saying something to somebody and you just don't know when they're going to attack you, or when it could cost you your life."

My flesh broke out in goosebumps. The lesson was for Uncle Bob, but it rooted itself inside me. This was one I would not have to learn the hard way.

At some point, the war between my parents reached some sort of detente. As my mother's words contained more spite and bile, he shut down—or perhaps he just gave up. When she knew he wasn't going to fight back, she stepped farther and farther over the line. I think he must have felt he deserved the verbal beating. Maybe he did. I don't know, but it was the surrendered dad I remember most.

But seeing him in defeat hurt my heart. No one should be so degraded. "Why do you take it?" one of us would ask him.

"I hurt your mom a lot," he'd say. "And I hurt her for a long time."

Eventually, her anger spilled over onto us. When Dad had fought back, she didn't have time to harangue us, but when she met no resistance and realized she was in control, she started fighting her kids and siblings.

Why are you yelling at me? I thought more than once. *I didn't do anything!*

My sister, Amber, would occasionally pick me up from school, but I generally walked, even on the coldest winter days. Amber and I were never close, but I knew that if I ran into a situation where I didn't feel safe, she would be there for me.

My dad was a certified welder and started working the night shift for TIC Welding, from 5 p.m. to 1 a.m. That only made things worse. Mom would call his job multiple times each night. "Where is he? Is he there?"

Nothing she could say or do stopped him from loving her.

My mother had her good days. She loved baking cakes, and she did her best to make our birthdays special. No matter how bad things got, I knew my mom would have my back. I attended University Park Elementary School from kindergarten to grade four. I was a straight-A student, but one day in grade four, I was called to a meeting with my teacher, my mother, and the principal. They told my mother that if I was going to continue into grade five, I would have to start taking Ritalin.

I was a distraction, they said. I wouldn't stop talking. Well, of course not! The assignments, especially math, were so easy that I would finish them in minutes, and then just sit there waiting for everyone else to catch up. Yes, I talked a lot, and yes, I probably had/have ADHD.

My mother said no - her kid was not going to be medicated. Maybe I was a pain in the ass, but I was creative and smart and she wasn't going to take that away from me.

"You just aren't challenging him enough," she said.

She moved me to Pineview Elementary, a special school with a gifted and talented program. Math became a dream class. Instead of doing fifth grade math that I could whiz through, they challenged me with more and more assignments until I was doing seventh grade math in my first year there. When I finished an assignment early, I could drop into another class and learn American Sign Language. The curriculum was the best medicine I could have asked for.

The biggest sun in my sky during those days was the Fowler family across the street. Their son, Jared, was my best friend. We were like brothers, utterly inseparable. I didn't have to pretend when I spent time with the Fowlers. They knew how dysfunctional we were. After school, I hung out at Jared's house. Anything was better than being home, and the Fowlers were the jackpot of better places to be. Their fridge was always full. They even had Mountain Dew and ordered food from Schwan's, and nothing was cooler than getting pizza and ice cream delivered by Schwan's.

They were my second family - my sane family - until the big falling-out when I was about twelve. Their oldest daughter, Sarah, told Amber she was going to run away. My mom got wind of it and called Mary-Jane Fowler, Sarah and Jared's mother, and then refused to let Sarah leave. Jared's parents came home, and we guessed Sarah lied about what was going on because somehow, both sets of parents blew up at each other.

The worst part of that scene was my parents' new edict: "You're not allowed to spend time with Jared anymore."

He was my best friend and my safe space! I still saw Jared, but I had to be careful to drift over there when my parents either weren't home or weren't watching. But the tension on the block was palpable.

I had another savior, and its name was baseball. From the time I could put on a mitt, I was at the sandlot down the street with Uncle Bob and his buddies.

They were seven or eight years older, but as long as I could be out there, I was happy. I found out that my dad had been a great baseball player when he was young, and immediately, I felt more connected to him. He'd make time to play catch with me, even if it was only for ten minutes before he went to work.

But he never made it to a single game in my entire childhood.

My buddy, Jesse McCauley's father, was a coach for an all-star team, and when Jesse found out how much I loved baseball, he talked to him. "Hey, Dad, I think Trapper's good enough to play for an all-star team. He hasn't played Little League, but could he try out?"

He said yes, and I got on a Little League team: the Milwaukee Brewers. I was ten and in kid heaven. After that, I tried out for Coach McCauley's team, The Hot Shots, and earned a place. From that point on, my life revolved around baseball. I was good. I played in the Hap Dumont World Series in 1995, a regional qualifier for the Little League World Series. I started off pitching and got utterly destroyed, giving up nine runs to a team from Ohio that only had eight players, but they were like men among boys. Even that couldn't put a damper on my enthusiasm. I met some lifelong friends that year: Josh Wadsorth, Chris Wren, Josh Elliot, and others. Those three are still in my life to this day and are great men.

My parents had no money for baseball gear. We depended on businesses sponsoring me, so my mother laid down strict rules. If I had a baseball game the next day, there'd be no sleepovers the night before. I was not allowed to bounce on a trampoline. As far as my mother was concerned, it was a death toy. She may not have been the best, but she let me know that if I made a commitment, I had to live up to it. I could not let my sponsors down. At the time, I don't think I understood her perspective, or even the full meaning of the word, "commitment," but it sunk into my mind, and I'm sure it shaped my character, because all my life, I've know that if i say I will do something, then I'll follow through. I didn't have to wait long to test my follow-through.

One day, my friend Josh asked me to a sleepover at his house. He had a pool and a trampoline. We had a game the next day, but I couldn't turn down what was such a big treat for me.

"Do you have a game tomorrow?" my mom asked when I went to her for permission.

"No."

She drove me across town and dropped me off. Josh and I stayed up late, and the next morning, we swam in the pool, jumped on the trampoline, and started a wrestling match while Phoenix, his big shepherd/chow dog, looked on. I fake-punched Josh, and Phoenix charged.

"Ow!"

I grabbed my scrotum. My hand was instantly drenched in blood.

Oh f**k!

I was twelve. What was this going to mean? Impotence? Would I still be able to be a father?

Josh was on the edge of panic. I called my father. "Dad - don't tell Mom, but I have a game later today and I just got bitten by a dog."

"How bad is it?" he asked.

"There's blood everywhere."

Dad got to the house in fifteen minutes, probably breaking every speed limit in the city. He drove me to the hospital. My mother arrived. Worried, of course, but also not happy that I'd lied to her.

The doctor assured us the bite wasn't deep; it was just in an area with many blood vessels. He applied Neosporin and a Band-Aid.

"What time's your game?" my mother asked.

"Five forty-five," I said. "But I'm not going to play."

She shook her head. "You lied to me, and yes, you're going to play. You made a commitment to your team."

I knew enough not to argue. I understood now that a commitment was my word, and my word had to be good. I played. In the second inning, I hit a ball to left center field, dove head first into second base, and tore off the Band-Aid, blood blooming out over my white uniform. Again, I remembered I'd made a commitment and played out the rest of the game.

One Saturday, I told my dad I wasn't a good hitter. With every pitch, I would step "out of the box" because I was afraid the ball might hit me. He took me to the sandlot and asked, "Do you trust me?"

"Yes."

He blindfolded me, put me in the batter's box, and walked to the mound. He had a great pitching arm. I heard the four or five fastballs he pitched whizzing by my ear. The next pitch he threw hit me right in the ribs. I pulled the bandana off my head, screaming and crying, "Why did you do that?"

I tore into the house, wiping snot off my face.

Dad followed behind me. "Did it hurt?"

"Yes!"

"Are you gonna live?"

"Well, yeah - I suppose."

He nodded. "From now on, every pitch that comes towards you, step into it and you'll become a hitter."

He was right. I learned a lot during those baseball years - about teamwork, having someone's back, and about what kept me interested. But even more, I learned about the importance of trust.

I discovered what I didn't want and how I didn't want to be. I never wanted a relationship where I couldn't rely on the other person. I wanted the security I'd never experienced. If my parents could treat me so badly, what would happen out there in the world, where no one even knew me? Was this just how everyone was? Were they going to be mean and only be out for themselves? I spent my childhood building a wall brick by brick, convinced I didn't need anyone on the other side. I could take care of myself, and that was exactly what I was going to do.

Perspective Shift

I used to think my childhood was just chaos. Just dysfunction. Just survival.

Now I see it as the forge where I learned how to hold on when everything inside me wanted to let go.

That little boy in the basement, face-to-face with a black widow spider... he became the man who now walks into the dark with other people, helping them feel safe enough to confront their own shadows.

I didn't grow up in a home that taught love the way love was meant to be shown. But I did learn loyalty. I learned endurance. I learned that even the people who hurt us the most can be deeply broken themselves—and that their pain doesn't have to become our identity.

I used to see my past as something I had to escape.

Now I see it as the foundation for everything I get to build.

This chapter wasn't written to point fingers. It's here to show you something important:

Your origin doesn't have to define your outcome.

No matter how your story started, you can rewrite how it ends.

You don't have to keep repeating what you were handed.

You get to choose what you pass on.

And even if love didn't look the way it was supposed to...

Even if safety was something you had to create for yourself...

Even if trust was a foreign language...

You're still allowed to want more.

You're still capable of healing.

You're still worthy of peace.

This is where the walls we built to survive finally begin to come down.

This is where self-protection becomes self-connection.

This is where the story shifts—from survival... to becoming.

You're not broken. You're being rebuilt.

Let's keep going.

— **Trapper**

CHAPTER 2

The Dawning of Awareness

On my first day at East Junior High, I met Seth Henley, and we became instant best friends. How does that work? You just sit there, start talking, and suddenly, you're inseparable. I spent a lot of time at Seth's house. If my parents asked where I'd been, the answer was always the same: "Seth's house."

"Well, why don't you bring Seth over here?"

I didn't want to. I was embarrassed to show him where and how I lived. But I couldn't avoid it forever, and when I finally did bring him home, he looked around and asked, "Where's your TV?"

"We don't have a TV."

At least that wasn't the worst thing about my house. It was different with Seth. The other kids I'd grown up with knew about my family - there was no need to hide anything. But Seth was new. How would he judge me?

I found out pretty quickly. Seth and his parents weren't the first people to tell me I stunk. I didn't shower. I don't think I'd ever showered. My father didn't shower. Maybe my mother did, but I couldn't be sure. No one had taught me about hygiene. I was the stinky kid, and until I entered junior high, I didn't know it. My clothes were hand-me-downs or from the second-hand store. The only new items I got were a couple of pairs of jeans from JCPenney and shoes from Payless.

JD and Marianne, Seth's parents, asked me, "How often do you shower?"

"I don't."

Maybe I should have been embarrassed, but I looked up to them, admired them, and they had just shown they cared about me enough to teach me about taking care of myself. Something inside me opened up to them. They saw me and accepted me for who I was. Seth told them about my house and my parents after he met them and saw them fight. Almost without my noticing, they stepped in to provide the guidance I'd never had. I could talk to them and they listened. If I mentioned girls or needed advice or feedback, they gave it. I felt safe bringing a girl to Marianne and JD's house when I felt uncomfortable bringing one to mine.

I spent more and more time away from home. I walked to school, walked home, and filled the long hours between being on the basketball team, the soccer team, the football team, playing baseball, and hanging out with friends. At thirteen, I was the kind of kid who was friends with everyone. I was a "good" kid. Teachers loved me, and probably no one was more surprised about that than they were. My aunt, uncle, and older sister had all attended the same schools. The teachers were prepared for someone who didn't care, blew off homework, and was only marking time. And there I was, straight A's and loving everything junior high could throw at me. I still talked a lot, but my teachers seemed pretty happy to overlook that.

At about that time, I also got the first clue that I might find some success as a businessman. Seth had a basketball hoop in his backyard, and I wanted one too. I told my mom and dad I wanted to save some money. I worked hard to get straight As - how about five dollars for every A? That would give me about thirty dollars with every report card. But a basketball hoop costs around $150. It snowed a lot in Casper, and I saw that as an opportunity. On weekends and on rare snow days when school was closed, I would walk around my neighborhood, knocking on doors and asking, "Hey, would you like me to shovel your walk?"

It didn't take long before I had about a hundred houses on a regular schedule. When it snowed, I took care of their walks and driveways, but that involved a lot of shoveling. So, I recruited Trevor and Travis, two young kids I deployed to strategic locations, paying them five dollars a house from the twenty I charged.

My sister, aunt, and uncle struck out on their own around this time, and it was just my parents and me. They were regular church-goers, and I'd always just tagged along. That changed when I began to understand what I was hearing and seeing, and concluded that there wasn't much to distinguish religion from government. In one, you had a priest; in the other, a president - both telling you what to believe. In one, you had tithing; in the other, taxes - both taking your money. Both institutions took pieces of your time, and both were focused on control. If they took your time and told you what to believe, you weren't thinking for yourself.

I began to look at the world around me more critically. As I spent more time with my friends' parents, particularly Seth's, I saw the full measure of my parents' dysfunction. Marianne and JD would argue, but those were friendly disagreements, not all-out war. If Seth or his little sister, Rachel, did something they shouldn't, Marianne and DJ talked to them. I was still getting spanked at age twelve because it was the only way my dad knew how to handle me if I got out of line. Sitting down and talking things out were not in his emotional toolbox.

I also had friends, like Josh, whose parents were divorced. Hanging out with him, his father, and his stepmom was great. Surely divorce was better than staying together on a battlefield.

I was still a kid when I began to understand that when you look back at your life, you should remember many more good times than bad. My sister and I remembered horrific times - far too many of them. One day, when my mother and father were screaming at each other again, I stepped in. "This is ridiculous! Get a divorce! I've seen people who divorced and remarried - and they're happy."

It was never going to happen. My dad loved my mother too much. Unfortunately, along with the love came equal amounts of resentment, distrust, and outright hate. I watched them struggle, realizing that I understood more about life at age thirteen than they did. And still, every Sunday, they went to church. And how was that making a difference? As far as I could see, the only thing the church was doing was taking their money, and there wasn't a penny to spare.

But they didn't trust the church either, and kept switching. Trust was nonexistent at our house. If it wasn't the church, then it was our relatives who were out to get us, or the neighbors, or our friends.

I learned a lot about relationships by observing my parents. Long before they said a word, I saw what they felt and what they were thinking by watching their eyes, or how they moved, sat, or positioned their bodies.

Thirteen was when many boys started flexing their muscles and going through growth spurts. Not me. I was still a "little kid"—about five feet two inches and less than a hundred pounds. When I went to Dr. Micholson for my annual physical, I asked, "Am I going to grow?"

"Don't worry about it," he said. "You'll grow when it's time for you to grow."

Seth was about my size, so I wasn't the only small kid in my class. I never got bullied, but I was picked on. It didn't really bother me. I liked everyone. I was a social kid, talking to everyone, smiling at folks, and greeting kids in the hall without reservation. But more and more, I became critical of how I looked. In gym class, we'd check our wingspan. A normal one was as wide as you were tall. Mine was at least eight inches wider. My fingertips fell below my knees. That was great for baseball - for any sport, really - but not for making me feel "normal."

The kids would call me "monkey" or "monkey arms." And to make things worse, I had huge feet. Being told I'd be big when I grew up didn't help.

The summer before high school, I got a job at Sears Roebuck, selling suits in the men's department, and I liked it a lot. First, because I enjoyed assisting people, and second, because I was helping myself. Thanks to Seth's parents, I'd literally cleaned up my act on the personal hygiene front - now I was learning about clothes beyond Goodwill and hand-me-downs. With my Sears discount,

I was able to stop looking completely weird. I also worked with people who were a few years older, who served as role models to some extent. And because I liked people, I received a nice share of customer service acknowledgments.

My coworkers were the first people I'd interacted with outside my circle. They came from different backgrounds; some were as young as I, others were in their fifties - a new world was opening up.

I also learned about rejection. In sales, people sometimes say no. And that was okay, too. I don't know where my confidence came from, but it was strong and unflappable.

Meanwhile, my parents would occasionally go out of town to work, leaving me alone at the house - a relief in many ways. In addition to being a welder, my dad was also a master mason who worked harder than anyone I've ever known. Because my mother didn't trust him, she was right there with him on the job. Because he was a welder, she got certified as a pipefitter. Because he was a mason, she also became a bricklayer. When he was called out of town for work, she went with him.

Every day, I grew more determined not to live a life like that. I knew I never wanted to communicate with my future wife the way they talked to each other. I didn't want to live in a house like theirs. I didn't want to work with my spouse all the time. I wanted a relationship where we were still our own persons. I was so clear about what I *didn't* want, but what *did* I want? All I knew for certain was that if I lived my life differently, I would find what I was after.

Perspective Shift

Awareness doesn't usually show up like lightning.

It sneaks in as discomfort. It whispers through contrast.

At thirteen, I didn't know I was waking up—but I was.

I didn't have the language for it, but I was beginning to see.

To question.

To unlearn.

I started to realize that the way I'd been raised wasn't the way I had to live.

That dysfunction didn't equal destiny.

That just because pain felt familiar didn't mean it was right.

For the first time, I understood that I had choices.

And with those choices came responsibility—not to be perfect, but to be conscious.

I saw what love looked like when it was healthy.

I saw what leadership looked like when it was quiet.

I saw what success could feel like when it wasn't rooted in survival.

And just like that, a question was born inside me that still guides me today:

"If I don't want what they had... what do I want instead?"

That's the question that changes everything.

Not "What am I running from?"—but "What am I walking toward?"

That's where the shift begins.

In the clarity.

In the courage.

In the decision to be the one who breaks the cycle.

Because someone has to go first.

And maybe, just maybe... that someone is you.

Let's keep going.

— **Trapper**

CHAPTER 3

Independence

The transition from junior high to high school was a big one. It was during that short time that I experienced trauma so big that I had to deal with it for years afterwards.

Entering tenth grade, I had another physical before joining the football team. I measured a whopping 5'2" and weighed in at 97 pounds. "I'm still the same size I was a year ago," I said. "My arms got longer, but I haven't grown or gained weight."

The doctor assured me I would grow.

However, my size was beginning to bother me, mainly due to Coach Keith, who was in charge of weightlifting for all grades, as well as football for the juniors and seniors. Seth and I were both at the low end of the weightlifting scale, but Coach Keith had requirements we had to meet, including pull-ups, push-ups, and the amount we could bench press. Weights were all new to me.

I faced my first bench press with Seth spotting me. The bar itself weighed ninety-five pounds - almost as much as me. And I was at another disadvantage: with my long arms, I would have to raise the bar far higher than anyone else, and then manage to bring it back down. Seth helped as much as he could, but five reps looked tougher than climbing Everest. Coach Keith watched, and by the time he turned away, I knew he didn't like me. I was a body language expert by then.

He believed I wasn't trying, and that was probably my biggest trigger. If my mother felt I wasn't making an effort, she would call me lazy. And I was never lazy. I loved to work hard. If I did something, I gave it a hundred percent.

"Lazy" was a lie! It wasn't me. For Coach Keith to believe or say I wasn't trying was negating who I was. I only wanted recognition, and Coach Keith was never going to give it to me.

And why did it matter to him whether or not I could bench press my body weight? I was a little guy. I wasn't about to play varsity. I wanted him to like me, just like I wanted everyone to like me. But nothing I could do would make that happen.

Luckily, I was on the freshman team, being coached by teachers who didn't care how big we were. Because I was so small, my mother had to sign a medical release, and that put the idea into the coaches' heads that I might get hurt. They didn't know how athletic, strong, and capable I really was. I could catch a ball with fingers as sticky as a lizard's tongue. They recognized it in practice, where I played on the scout team or practice team, and I dominated every time. We'd get merit stickers every week, and by the time I was in my junior year, my helmet was plastered with them. There wasn't a clear inch to spare. Anyone seeing that helmet, and not the helmet's owner, would think it belonged to the captain of the team, or at least to someone enshrined in the hall of fame.

But they still wouldn't put me into a competitive game because they were afraid I'd be injured. The only thing that got injured that season was my pride when some big guys grabbed me and Brad, another pretty small guy, after practice and taped us to the same bench - me upside down underneath it and Brad on top. Brad and I talked a lot - enough to be pretty annoying, so we probably deserved some minor hazing.

Joe Miller, a junior who was a bit of a slacker, had taken a liking to me and cut us loose when he found our taped-up bodies. After that, he quietly looked out for me. He was just popular enough that if he told someone to leave me alone, they would.

About halfway through the season, I got my big break. We were playing a team in Gillette, Wyoming, when our two best receivers got injured. Sure, I felt bad for them, but my overriding sense was unbridled excitement - here was my chance to play! And I killed it. I played out the rest of the season, and I was good - better than anyone could have hoped for.

At the sports awards at the end of the year, head coach Stafalino called me up on the stage before the prizes were handed out. "We need to recognize Trapper," he said. "Who knew that he was so athletic? We never gave him a shot, but when we did, we immediately wished we'd let him play the whole year. We saw his spirit, his energy, his athleticism, and his willingness to work harder than anybody else."

My heart grew two sizes. Even the seniors in the crowd nodded at me in appreciation.

The recognition had the added benefit of giving me more respect as I entered my junior year.

Then, my buddies started dating. Seth and Josh both had girlfriends. I wanted that too, but every girl I asked to go to the movies or to just hang out said no. No amount of rejection could stop me. I just kept asking. It was their loss because they had no idea what a great guy I actually was. And besides, no one was more special than anyone else. Seth and Josh still included me, probably putting their girlfriends on notice right from the start: "Hey, Trapper is going to be around a lot because his family sucks."

When I showed up, no one seemed to mind.

And then I got a girlfriend just before my junior year. A friend talked to his dad, who gave me a summer and after-school job at Overhead Door that paid almost twice what I'd pulled in at Sears Roebuck. My friend's dad, the owner, had a daughter, Stephanie, who worked in the office when she wasn't attending Gonzaga College in Spokane, Washington. She was four years older, and I thought she was pretty cute. When I asked her out, she said yes.

We spent a lot of time together, but she was twenty-one and could go to bars, and when she did, I couldn't help but wonder, "What is she doing tonight? Who's she with?"

Despite my misgivings, we stuck together.

Football season started at the end of August, and now Keith was my coach. I still couldn't lift weights, and would show up for attendance and leave. My sanctuary was Mrs Sally Oates' physical education class. She loved teaching PE and accepted everyone for who they were, letting them play and train to their abilities. She knew I wasn't supposed to be there, but she never said a word. Coach Keith didn't even notice I wasn't in the weight room, because if you weren't a starter, he didn't see you. He didn't care where you lived, or about your home life, or even if you were human.

At an early practice, I was running fast backwards and tripped over a sprinkler head protruding from the ground. I fell, sustaining a Lisfranc sprain characterized by hundreds of microfractures in the foot. The players watching were confused. Why did I fall? Puzzled, Coach Horn walked over. Ah - a sprinkler head! I hadn't been faking it!

The trainer wrapped up my foot so I could stay in practice. Yes, it hurt, but I was determined to keep playing. I attended every practice. I was only on the scout team, but I loved every minute of it, even running across the field, the quarterback tossing the ball to me, the big two-hundred-pound guys tracking me down, thumping me to the ground.

I ran harder and faster, caught the ball, and kept coming back for more. Everything I did, I did as hard as I could, putting every piece of my heart and soul into it.

Not every gym class was about weightlifting. If we were playing arena football, I didn't skip class, and Coach Keith always picked me for his team because he knew I had talent and I would catch the ball without dropping it, not once. But he never put me into a real game. I guessed he was punishing me for not lifting - or just penalizing me for some reason I was unaware of.

In October, I went hunting with my mother and father, as we did every year. I let Coach Keith know, just in case. His strict rule was that if you missed an unexcused practice or arrived late without permission, you would be removed from the team. We headed for an area outside Big Piney, Wyoming, towing a rickety trailer my father had built from the bed of an old pickup truck. We bagged two cow elk that weekend and headed home on Sunday, but were sidelined when an axle broke. I knew immediately I wouldn't make it to practice on Monday.

Someone eventually stopped and helped us get to the next town, where a garage fixed the trailer. We were on the road again Monday morning. The minute we pulled up in front of our house, I raced to the school, running around the side, and tearing down the hill to the field where practice had started seventeen minutes earlier. I guessed if I hadn't shown up, Coach Keith wouldn't have missed me for a minute.

But I was supposed to be there, so I ran, the other players and coaches watching. Gasping for air, I pulled up on the field.

"Trapper," Coach Keith yelled. "You're late for practice. You weren't excused. Turn in your shit."

I stopped breathing. "What? Are you serious?"

"You're not excused. You're tardy. You're done. You're off the team."

I didn't say the words that flooded my mind. "I'm not even important to you. I don't even play. I show up every day, and I do everything I'm supposed to do as hard as I can. Why is it important to you to kick an insignificant person off the team?" He had no idea what he took away from me.

At that moment, I shrank another two inches. I was less important than a cockroach. He took something away from me that day. More than that, he erased my sanctuary.

Without a word of protest, I turned and ran back up the hill and into the locker room, where I turned in my helmet, my gear, and my prized jersey. We'd been given new jerseys that year. I had my name on the back. I'd never had that, and I had to turn it in.

On some level, I knew the significance of that moment - that my life was about to change. In my heart was a lump of grief; on my face, I was giving nothing away. I knew I couldn't plead with him. He didn't care. Unless I could advance his career in some way, I was worthless to him.

I called my mom. "Hey, Coach Keith just kicked me off the football team." I went to a party a few days later with Seth, Josh, and a few other friends. Half the football team was there, getting hammered. On Monday, I heard that a few of them didn't make it to school and even missed practice. Two players were even charged as a minor in possession (MIP). None of them were kicked off the football team.

When my mother found out, you could see the steam blowing out of her ears. She took me to the principal's office and tore into him and Coach Keith. It didn't make a difference - maybe even worsened the situation. She wasn't doing it right! I could have said it so much better. Maybe I could make them understand how much I wanted and needed to be on that team. Coach Keith was taking everything important away from my life: structure, discipline, community - he was ripping out a piece of my heart, and I would never be the same.

With my refuge gone, I had too much time on my hands - time I didn't want to spend at home. I started hanging out with Mike Myler, a guy I'd been playing baseball with for years. He drank and smoked weed, so I hung out with him and some other baseball friends. They weren't the best influence, but I had a car by then, and I had a job, and I figured I could do what I wanted. I organized my school schedule so I could start at 7 a.m., get off at 1 p.m., and work from 2 p.m. to 6 or 7 p.m.

That's when my parents took a job out of town for about six months, leaving me on my own. When they came back and found out I was still dating Stephanie, they weren't happy. My mother laid into me about having a girlfriend, especially an older one. And what about sex?

The truth was, we fooled around, but we still hadn't gone that far. One time, when Stephanie came over to the house and my mother was being as bitchy as only she could be, Stephanie took up my cause. "You're being terrible to Trapper," she said, and, turning to me, "Trapper - you've got a job. Just move out."

When she left, my dad gave me an ultimatum - she goes or you do.

"I'm better off without you," I said, gathered up my stuff, and moved into a run-down studio apartment on Second Street across from the Sinclair gas station. I was genuinely on my own.

Perspective Shift

Independence isn't just about moving out.

It's about waking up to the fact that no one's coming to save you—and realizing... maybe that's your greatest opportunity.

In this season of my life, I didn't feel strong. I felt discarded, overlooked, and misunderstood. I wanted to scream, "See me!" to coaches, parents, girls, God—anyone. I didn't want applause. I just wanted to matter.

What I didn't know then—but understand now—is that the most powerful people you'll ever meet are the ones who had to learn how to believe in themselves when no one else did.

When Coach Keith kicked me off that team, he didn't just take my jersey. He took my identity. At least, that's what I thought.

But the truth is... he freed me from ever needing his validation again.

That loss became a line in the sand: You will not define me.

From that day forward, I started becoming someone new.

Not a victim. Not just a survivor.

But someone who knew how to rebuild from scratch.

That's the kind of independence that can't be handed to you—it has to be earned.

And once you've earned it, no one can ever take it away.

So if you've been overlooked, underestimated, or thrown aside...

Know this:

There's a fire in your pain. And it's shaping who you're becoming.

You may not be where you want to be yet.

But you're no longer who you were.

Let's keep going.

— **Trapper**

CHAPTER 4

Betrayal and Loss

My apartment was basic. I could enter it through the front door and down a long hallway where the bare overhead light bulbs were either burned out or flickering, or via the back, covered stairway, which was dark, cold, and rickety.

I'd walk into a box of a room - my bed at the far end, a small bathroom past that, and a tiny kitchen on one wall. That was it. But it was quiet and mine. Every time I walked in, knowing it was my own space, I felt the weight lift from my shoulders. No one was shouting or throwing dishes, and no one was monitoring my life. I did have a weird neighbor across the hall. One day, I came home from work to find him poking around in my apartment. How did he get in?

"I have a key for all the apartments," he said.

After it happened a couple more times, I called the landlord, who assured me the man was strange but harmless. I changed the locks. Having a neighbor poking into my space wasn't going to do anything to tamp down my anxiety attacks. I'd been having them for a while, but was unwilling to deal with them. When I had a bout, it felt like a boulder falling into my soul. I couldn't breathe. I was going to die.

One day at work, I was convinced that I was the world's most massive failure. My life was ending. The weight smothered me, my head spun, and I vomited. I finally went to my doctor.

"What you described is a massive anxiety attack," he said.

What should I do about them?

I knew there were going to be more. I couldn't avoid them because I constantly felt like I was letting someone down and not meeting their expectations. It was never about me – always about others. But I didn't know what their expectations were. I invented them and made assumptions about some impossibly high standards I couldn't meet.

I think at the time that's what anxiety was: making assumptions about how someone perceives us, but we don't know – we're just guessing, and that leads to chaos in our minds.

After my doctor talked to me, I knew then I could no longer let it slide. I had to be able to work and live my life. He prescribed a low dose of Xanax. The drug made me perpetually tired, but it also staved off the attacks.

With the newfound freedom I had, I could have gone right off the rails, but I'd already had a taste of it when my parents were away, and I wasn't interested in ruining my life. I understood responsibility. I had a job, a car, and a girlfriend I was in love with. Everything I did, I did for her. I spent as much time at her house as I did in my little flat - and I was determined to prove to her parents, and probably the whole world, that I was good enough to deserve her and everything that came with that commitment.

It didn't occur to me that I could drop out of school and become a party boy. I focused on my education and my work. My future was so certain, I didn't even think about it. All I had to do was work hard at Overhead Door for Stephanie's parents, climb the ladder to success, and be the best employee I was capable of being. It was a simple, straightforward road to a normal life. Stephanie's parents had a nice house and a good life.

I'd never paid attention to people's houses until I met Seth, and then, Oh! Their house was tidy and clean, and they had a garage. They were probably wealthy. That looked like success. Then I saw Stephanie's parents' house on a big property with a two-car garage and new vehicles inside it. They had their own business. This was a new benchmark for me: a higher level of success, and I wanted the same.

Seth and I were still best friends, but he and Josh were involved with girlfriends and school. I was more focused on work and hanging out with

Stephanie, watching movies or just talking. One thing we didn't talk about was the future. Maybe I was still too young, or maybe I simply took our future together for granted. Or was I afraid that her vision of our future was different from mine?

I graduated with a 3.8 GPA. Surprisingly, my parents hosted a small graduation party for Seth, Josh, and me. It felt a bit awkward because it was just our small trio, our parents, and some of my parents' friends. Were they showing me they were proud? In their own way, they were probably demonstrating love. I doubt I grasped that at the time.

Most of my friends headed off to college. I had a couple of baseball scholarships and could have gone, but I was in love, and I had a job and a car payment and grown-up responsibilities. I was too invested in my life to give up a single piece of it. I enrolled in Casper Community College to become a PE teacher, inspired by Sally Oates, whose classes I had escaped to when I walked out of the weightlifting room every week. Besides, I liked kids, and teaching anything physical just had to be fun.

I quickly discovered that my motivation to graduate from high school didn't carry through to college. I'd always believed that a high school degree was a must. I didn't question that any more than I doubted gravity. But college just didn't inspire that same feeling, or anything even remotely like it. Maybe if I'd believed college was mandatory, I would have done better, but it felt more like an afterthought. I was working more, making more money, and beginning to doubt my direction at college. And then I spoke with one of my professors, who informed me that as a PE teacher, I could expect to earn between $16,000 and $20,000 a year.

What? I was making double that already at Overhead Door!

I may have liked the idea of being a PE teacher, but I'd grown up in poverty. I saw what that did to a family and how it limited your choices. I wanted to provide well for my future family.

I wanted what Stephanie's parents, Roy and Joanne, had – a nice house in a good neighborhood, and their own business.

I left college and dedicated myself to Overhead Door, certain it would lead me to the future I envisioned.

One day, I had a doctor's appointment and arrived at a customer's house a few minutes late.

"I'm sorry," I said.

She waved off my apology, gave me a sweet smile, and watched me inspect her garage door. By then, I'd been working with Overhead Door long enough I could diagnose a problem just by listening and detecting noises a door shouldn't make and the sounds it made when it was operating properly. I pushed the remote, concentrating carefully.

"You know," I said. "I think you need new end bearings and some rollers. You're getting a lot of noise here and here."

She gave me a broad smile. "You went to the doctor to get diagnosed, and now you're doing the diagnosis. You're like the garage doctor."

Oh...

Back in my car, I wrote the name down in a sketchbook I kept with me. Underneath the name, I doodled a little stethoscope. Maybe someday I could own a company...

Not long after that, another customer called me "The Door Whisperer." Another note in my little sketchbook.

Other changes after high school also had a significant impact. While my friends went off to college to play baseball, I wasn't playing for the first time since I'd discovered the game. Two words: it sucked. But I was also suddenly living a fully adult life, and the last pieces of childhood fell away as I poured myself into work, drinking, and partying when I had some free time.

By the time I graduated, I'd grown to about 5'6", and then shot up to 5'10" the following summer. I was still pretty lean at about 125 pounds, but I had a hard time seeing myself as anything other than tiny.

Even recently, I was talking with another soccer dad, telling him how small I was.

"It's crazy you would think like that," he said. "You're a big dude."

"I don't feel like a big dude."

Sure, I know I'm a good size, and I've got muscles, but I can look at a guy my size and think *he's bigger than I am*. Something deep inside me sees a sixteen-year-old runt. I don't let it stop me from living a great life, but that kid is still in there, with all his insecurities. He's still little. When people see you as a little guy, they expect you to play small and be small. I felt like I constantly had to compete and prove myself. I've covered my body with tattoos, and they look great, but they also hide my skin, and maybe they make me feel bigger.

When I was young, I thought I was so small that people couldn't see me. Oh sure, they could see my body, but what about *me*? Could they recognize the person inside me who wanted to belong, be acknowledged, and loved? Coach Keith couldn't see me! He couldn't see what he was missing out on! Could anyone see that?

The rejection still aches today, but now I want people to see themselves. That's my mission. I want everyone to realize how special they are. Being acknowledged is so important, and perhaps most important of all, is the acknowledgement we give ourselves.

I was nineteen when I moved from my dingy apartment into a house with three buddies, including Jared, my childhood best friend. In an instant, it became a party house. That worked fine for my friends - they were all in college. However, I had to get up every morning and go to work six days a week, generally arriving on the job by 6:30 or 7 a.m. Sure, I wanted to party, but my job was the bigger priority.

I was the youngest in the house, but I was the adult. When I chose my bedroom, I picked the one whose window looked into a garage, reasoning I could sleep better with less light to disturb me. But the living room was on the other side of my door, and on a Wednesday or Thursday night I'd be yelling, "Can you guys just shut the fuck up! I'm trying to sleep!"

I was taking my life seriously - maybe too seriously. I was responsible. I had a car payment, rent to pay, credit cards, a job to go to and excel at. I didn't have time for unbridled fun. On many nights, I would go to Stephanie's house, just so I could sleep. I'd get up in the morning and walk into the kitchen where her father, Roy, would be making coffee. He'd pour a cup for each of us, and then we'd drive to work in separate cars.

After about a year, I moved out of the house and into a nice one-bedroom apartment in a good building. Peace and quiet at last. Stephanie came over more often, and that was great. Or was it? We'd said "I love you," and I'd even talked to Roy about marrying her. I was all in. We spent a lot of time with Brian Sorensen and his girlfriend, Jessica. We had some good couple dates, but as time went on, there were fewer of those. Stephanie became more distant, and she started picking fights, often over nothing. What was going on? As our disagreements became more frequent, I felt like an angry badger was gnawing on my stomach.

One night, feeling even more anxious than usual, I made the call. No answer. Okay, I knew she was out at a bar with her friends, and I was still not twenty-one, so here I was. Alone. At home. I called again. Straight to voicemail. At midnight, I called her mother. "Is everything all right with Stef? I can't get a hold of her."

A pause. "You know, maybe you guys just need some space. Maybe she's just having fun with people her age."

A couple of days later, Brian knocked on my door. "Trap, everyone knows what's happening. You're blind to it. I hate to be the one to tell you, but Stephanie's seeing another guy."

What?

The pain was physical - right through my body. Stephanie? No! I loved her! I was going to marry her!

But hadn't Seth and Josh been hinting at something? I thought they were talking BS. If it was true, then everyone knew but me.

I didn't want to believe it. I had to see it. Brian obliged. He had an idea where the guy lived. "You didn't hear it from me," he said. "But here's his address."

I drove there with Jared. I needed emotional support on this one. I knocked on the door. A twelve-year-old boy opened it.

"Hey," I said, pretty sure I had the wrong house. "Who are you?"

"Who are you?" he replied.

"My name's Trapper. I'm looking for Stephanie. Her car's out front."

A man walked up behind the boy, and right beside him was Stephanie. The guy was at least ten or fifteen years older than her.

I looked at Stephanie. "Dude - for real? He's got a kid half your age!"

I spun around, blinking back tears, got in the car, and drove away.

I couldn't leave her-not completely. At work the next day, there she was. Every time I saw her, my heart cracked in half all over again. I put my head down and worked.

Then, one night at about 1 a.m., I woke up to the sound of a car horn blaring in the apartment parking lot below my bedroom window. I stumbled out of bed to the window in my boxers and looked down. In the pool of light was Stephanie, teetering drunkenly beside her car, leaning on her horn.

I rushed down. "Hey! What's up? You shouldn't be driving. Come up and I'll call your mom."

She pushed me off, muttering, yelling - so drunk I couldn't understand her. I called Roy. "Stephanie's here and she's losing it. She's kicking my car. You'd better come and get her. She's drunk."

I wasn't the only one awake. Others had heard the commotion and called the police. A cruiser pulled up, and a female police officer got out.

Oh fuck.

I'd grown up with this scene. I knew what to expect. The optics were working heavily against me.

The officer said, "Sir, I need you to step over to the car."

"I'm glad you're here," I said. "She's intoxicated."

"Stay here."

She turned to Stephanie. "Did he hit you?"

"I was asleep," I said. "Her mom and dad are on the way."

A second cruiser pulled up. Another woman officer got out who pulled my arms back and put me in cuffs.

Then Roy arrived in his big Ford truck.

"Hey, Roy," I said. "This situation is crazy. Someone called the cops 'cause she was screaming."

He turned to one of the cops. "Why is Trapper in cuffs?"

"It was reported as a domestic dispute. This is just protocol. If there's a man on site and the police responding are women, we put them in cuffs just for everyone's safety."

The other officer added, "There's a belief that he may have hit her."

"But she said I didn't hit her!" I protested.

Roy said, "Trapper would never hit her."

How the incident was resolved is a blur because that was my "coming to Jesus" moment. That was not how I wanted my life to go. I had to make a change—not next week or next month—right then.

The next day, I called my sister, who had moved to Denver with her husband, Trevor. "Can I come and live with you guys? I need to get out of Casper."

Ron, Roy's brother and my immediate boss, offered me double my salary to stay. I hadn't had a raise in three years, and now he was going to pay me twice what he had been?

I packed up and left. If I wasn't going to be valued here for who I was, then I needed to get out and become a different person. If they couldn't see my worth, then I would determine my own value. In fact, I was going to create a whole new me.

Perspective Shift

Some betrayals don't break us.

They reveal us.

At the time, I thought the pain would destroy me.

And in a way, it did.

But not in the way I feared.

The man I was—the one who needed approval, needed to be chosen, needed someone else to complete him—he didn't survive.

Because in his place, a different version of me was born.

One who realized that love doesn't equal loyalty...

That effort doesn't guarantee security...

And that even the deepest commitment won't keep someone who's already left you in their heart.

Heartbreak forced me to do something I'd never done before:

Choose myself.

Not because I didn't love her.

But because I finally understood that I'd been giving all of myself to people who hadn't earned the right to hold it.

I had spent years trying to prove I was enough for someone else's dream.

But I'd never stopped to ask:

What's my dream? Who do I want to become?

Leaving Casper wasn't just a move—it was a declaration.

I was done waiting to be seen.

I was done letting pain define me.

If you've been left, lied to, or looked over—this is your moment too.

Not to get revenge.

Not to prove your worth.

But to reclaim your life.

You don't have to earn your way back to being whole.

You already are.

Let's keep going.

— **Trapper**

CHAPTER 5

Party Boy

I piled my stuff into my little Subaru Impreza and drove to Parker, Colorado, a suburb of Denver. For the next month, I threw myself a giant pity party until my sister, Amber, had had enough.

"You need to get a job," she said. "You need to start supporting yourself, and you need to start contributing."

She wasn't wrong. I had to get my shit together.

Right. I showered, shaved, combed my hair, put on a long-sleeved blue shirt, khaki pants, and black dress shoes, and drove to Arapaho Road, the car dealership street. From one end to the other, you could buy anything from a Toyota Corolla to a Dodge Ram.

I pulled into the John Elway Dodge dealership because it was the closest one. If they didn't hire me, a long line of others stretched out as far as I could see. I was sure I'd hit a home run in one of them. I walked to the front entrance and approached the man standing there, reaching out my hand. "Hey there, my name is Trapper. I'm your new car salesman. I'm supposed to start today."

He laughed - a big, full-bodied roar. "I like your attitude. I'm Jim Bauman, the general manager. We didn't hire anybody, but come on inside. I'll get you an application and we'll start your training today."

The truth is, they probably would have hired anyone. It was a car dealership! But I think my confidence gave me an edge. Where did that confidence come from? Partly from the new persona I was creating, and partly because I'd almost always had it. No one knew me in this city. I had no history here. I could be anyone I wanted to be, so why not create someone entirely different from the anxious little kid I'd been in Casper? I could be a bad boy. I could be a party boy. Hell, I could be a lady's man if that's what I wanted. And for sure, I could be the best salesperson Arapahoe Road had ever seen.

Within sixty days, I was one of the top performers at the dealership. Suraj Talabi, one of my mentors, went beyond teaching me sales techniques - he also decided to look out for me, trying to steer me away from the hardest partiers in the shop. Though he did his best, I fell in with them. I also made friends with Devin Draper, a unique character from Iowa who was more even-keeled. He was a good friend to me, and we still stay in touch to this day. But the "new me" went out on Friday nights, and sometimes during the week, getting so drunk so often, that a lot of that time has become a blur with no clear memories of events.

I was spending a lot of money, but I was also earning a pile of cash. I can recall getting a six-thousand-dollar bonus one Friday because I'd sold a lot of cars that week. In the six months I worked there, I averaged fifteen thousand dollars a month.

One night, a bunch of us from the Subaru store, the Ram store, and my store walked into a dive bar where I got absolutely destroyed. I will never know how I made it home in my car. My sister woke me up at 10 a.m. the next morning, and I was still drunk, smelling like a distillery.

"Jim called the house," she said. "You're supposed to be at work. There's a deal you're supposed to do. Oh - and you can't live here anymore. You're making a ton of money, and you're not contributing. You have to get your own place."

Again, my sister wasn't wrong.

I dragged myself out of bed, tucked my rumpled, stinky shirt into my pants, and got behind the wheel of my car. During that two-mile drive to the dealership, I pulled over three times to vomit at the side of the road. At the store, I pulled into a handicapped spot just because it was closest to the door and stumbled inside, looking like I had just left the club.

Melissa, the customer, was waiting for me. I pulled myself together, trying to present a professional appearance, but minutes after greeting her, I had to say, "I'll be with you in a second. I just have to go to the bathroom."

I threw up again. Jim followed me in. "Trapper," he said. "You have a problem. When you're working here, if we notice someone struggling with alcohol or drugs, we have a responsibility to try to help them."

I sold the car to Melissa with the help of a colleague, and then I walked into Jim's office.

"If you want, you can quit your job," he said. "But I have to offer you the help of an alcohol advisor."

I nodded. "Okay. Whatever we have to do."

Jim signed me up for Alcoholics Anonymous, where I had to go to meetings and talk with my advisor twice a week. I wasn't what you'd call a dedicated reformee, but I knew I had to get my drinking under control. If I stayed on the path I was on, I'd ruin my life.

The persona I'd created when I moved to Denver was not me. He was someone I had invented, and he was walking down a dangerous road. In my heart, I was still the same person I had always been, and he was a good person. But when I left Wyoming, I didn't want to be good. That person had been ignored, undervalued, and hurt once too often. I wanted to be one of the bad boys who swaggered down the street, challenges and bad days sliding off him like Teflon.

But now, drunk and hungover, I saw that I was in danger of becoming the persona I'd invented and letting the real me slip away. And besides, I could never truly inhabit the bad boy image. I liked the idea of being an asshole because the asshole always won. But those wins were short-term. In the long run, winning meant being me.

One day, I was having lunch with my sponsor, who also worked in the John Elway dealership network. He told me, "When I recovered, I was young too. You're going to be around alcohol for a long time, especially in social settings. For me, it wasn't about quitting drinking - it was about regulating it and understanding my relationship with it."

In AA, I learned that a lot of guys drink to lower their inhibitions and feel more comfortable in social situations. I had no problems with that when I was sober. That wasn't why I drank. I actually didn't like the taste of alcohol, and I absolutely didn't like being hungover. So why did I drink? The answer seemed clear: it was part of my new persona that no longer served me.

With some self-examination, I was able to establish a healthier relationship with alcohol. I didn't need it. More importantly, drinking would cost me opportunities to live the life I wanted. Both Seth's and Stephanie's parents had shown me that if I lived my life authentically and worked hard, I would be successful. But what did success mean? In Casper, it looked like a beautiful house with a two-car garage. Working at the dealership, it had come to mean making thousands of dollars a month. But my definition of success was evolving. I was beginning to see it as a life of service to others. But first, I also had to be in service to myself. If I kept drinking, I would be no good to anyone else, let alone myself.

Jim Bauman saved my life. Even after I stopped working for his dealership, I continued to drop by. He and the group of guys there had become a sort of family, with Jim taking on the role of an uncle-like figure.

I knew that one way to get myself sorted out was to get back to what I'd been doing so well. I wouldn't be making as much money, and maybe that would be a good thing. I called Ron, my former boss at Overhead Door of Casper, and asked him to provide a referral to Overhead Door in Denver.

Based on my experience and Ron's recommendation, they hired me, and things began to fall into place. It felt familiar, and I was good at what I did. I was living with Chris, a young guy I had become friends with at the dealership who was responsible, didn't drink, and was a great fit for me. My work hours were reasonable again. I was on track.

One day, we had a team meeting. I was sitting at the end of a row in a room of about fifty people when Robert Pettyjohn, one of the owners of the operation, walked in. As he passed me, I looked down and then up at him. "Hey, Bob. Those are some sweet boots!"

"They'd better be pretty sweet for forty thousand dollars," he said.

Wow, I thought. *What a piece of shit!* To say that in front of a bunch of guys who couldn't afford to buy a house, all working for him, doing their best to make ends meet.

I was an area leader in charge of other technicians. As a certified overhead door technician, I trained other technicians and helped them become more efficient and productive. One day, Pettyjohn called me into his office. "Hey, I've been looking at your numbers," he said. "One thing I noticed is that you talk a lot."

"Yes, I do talk a lot," I said. "I like to build relationships."

"Man, I think you could get another job or two done if you didn't talk so much."

I looked at him long and hard. "When I'm talking a lot, I'm building your business. I'm not building my business. I'm creating opportunities for you and your company. I could very well do that for myself."

What did I just say? Am I listening to myself? Why am I working for this rich a-hole?

I walked out of his office and quit my job. Then I called my brother-in-law, Trevor, because he was the smartest man I knew. "Hey, do you know how to start a business?"

"Why?"

"I think I'm going to start my own company. If this guy who owns forty-thousand-dollar boots can run a company, I think I can do it too. I'm pretty sure I'm smarter than him."

Perspective Shift

Sometimes the person we pretend to be shows up...

And almost steals the life we were born to live.

I created a persona the moment I left Casper.

Cool. Confident. Party-hard.

I thought I was building freedom.

But really, I was building a mask—one drink, one late night, one lie at a time.

I wanted to feel powerful.

But I was only powerful when I was me.

Even your lowest version can lead you back to your highest self—if you're willing to listen.

That hangover didn't just make me sick.

It shook me awake.

The guy getting drunk on Friday nights and vomiting in parking lots wasn't me.

He was a response. A reaction. A decoy.

And deep down, I knew it.

Because no matter how many people I made laugh, or how many sales I closed, I still wanted something more:

Peace. Purpose. A path that actually felt like mine.

This is where I stopped trying to be liked by everyone...

And that's what I want for you, too.

Not perfection.

Not image.

Just you, raw and real and radically honest.

Because once you meet yourself again,

You'll never go back to pretending.

Let's keep going.

— **Trapper**

CHAPTER 6

The Garage Doctor

On September 1, 2005, I registered *The Garage Doctor LLC* with the Secretary of State for Colorado, a full-service garage door company doing sales, service, and installations. I was twenty-two and I had my own company! I was an entrepreneur! I even had a company vehicle: a 1990 two-tone brown Ford F350 crew cab long bed truck with a cracked windshield. It wasn't much to look at, but it got me to the job sites.

Trevor helped me get my proverbial ducks in a row. He told me I needed a scale tag, meaning I had to get my truck weighed because it was now a commercial vehicle. I found a nearby company, Santa Fe Sand and Gravel, that could do the job for me.

I drove down and walked into the office, where a man and a woman were reviewing some papers. "Hey," I said, excitement and pride spilling out of my pores. "My name is Trapper. I just started a company, and I need to get a scale tag."

Sure," they said. "We can do that. It's ten dollars."

The woman, who introduced herself as Ashley and her husband, Dave, asked, "What kind of business did you just start? We're entrepreneurs, and we think it's exciting when someone starts out on their own."

"It's called The Garage Doctor," I said. "I do garage door installations and anything related to garage doors."

"Oh," she said. "We just put an addition on our home. Would you like to bid on the project?"

"Absolutely!"

Was I excited? Internally, I must have been vibrating. The memory of that moment brings tears to my eyes. Ashley and Dave Moore had no idea who I was. They had never met me. And yet, they were willing to take a chance on an enthusiastic young guy of twenty-two, which changed my life.

I followed Dave's car to their house, situated on impressive acreage, where they had just built an oversized two-car garage that would require two eighteen-by-eight garage doors.

Holy shit, I thought. *This is going to be my first gig? This is huge!*

I didn't quite believe I'd been given this opportunity, but I was determined to put in the winning bid and then do the best job I'd ever done.

I'm sure I bid around six thousand dollars for both doors and probably made no more than four hundred in profit. Seth helped me with the job due to its size. Since that first job with Ashley and Dave, I've upgraded their doors twice, and in the process, Dave has become a friend and mentor. They were instrumental in helping me launch The Garage Doctor and setting me on the road to success.

Then they introduced me to the owner of Maaco, an auto body shop, who needed some servicing work done at the shop and a new door at his house. "Dave said you did an amazing job for him," he told me. "He said you're a young guy, and we want to support your growth."

After I completed the work, he handed me an envelope with my check. "There's a little something extra in there," he said. "By the way, that's the ugliest truck I've ever seen."

"I know," I said. "But it's all I could afford, and it gets the job done."

"I'll bet it would look better if it was all white," he said.

"I'll bet it would," I agreed.

I opened the envelope. Along with my check, it contained a voucher for a paint job and a new windshield.

I was excited, not by the money or the unexpected bonus, but by the fact that two successful men had recognized my value. I believed, even then, that taking care of people meant they would take care of you. Even as a child, I wanted to make people proud of me. I didn't have the positive reinforcement I craved at home and worked hard to get it out in the world. I believed I could create value by providing excellent service and exceeding expectations.

I'd always known I was good with people, but my first few months in business proved it to me. I also trusted myself. I knew that if I got a job, I would do it right and make my customers happy.

In those early days, I had no money for advertising or marketing. I had business cards printed at Office Depot and ordered a couple of Garage Doctor shirts. When I wasn't busy with a job, I walked around neighborhoods, knocking on doors and offering free evaluations. If no one was home, I'd tape a card to the front door and another on their garage door. I targeted my sister's neighborhood first because she knew people, and people knew her. I could tell them she'd give me a referral.

I had no ambitions to create a large company with numerous employees; I just wanted to take care of myself and pay my bills. And those were good months. I still partied and drank—but a lot less. I had a pretty good group of friends from a softball team I had joined called "ICEMEN." I had a business and Gunner, so I had to be responsible.

Gunner was the pup I adopted just before leaving the car dealership, and he was the best dog. In fact, I'd say he saved me. When I left the dealership and went back to Overhead Door, even though I'd gone through the AA program, I was still sincerely concerned that I'd kill myself with drinking and partying. I had just adopted Gunner when I went to a party with a buddy. We walked in with two girls we'd picked up at a bar. Lines of cocaine were drawn out on the kitchen table. The girls walked straight over and snorted a couple of lines. That's when I knew I shouldn't be there. And I needed to take care of Gunner.

But I didn't make it home. I slept in the parking lot of the supermarket next door and walked fifteen miles home the next morning to Gunner, who'd been home alone all that time. It took a while for me to become a responsible dog owner, but I did - and he saved me. I should have been taking care of him, but Gunner took care of me.

He continued to be there for me when I started Garage Doctor. He taught me about being responsible, not only to him, but also to my business and my clients.

I was really getting myself into shape, and then, only a couple of months after becoming an entrepreneur, I met Sam.

Perspective Shift

This wasn't just the chapter where I started a business. This was the chapter where I started believing in myself.

The Garage Doctor was never just a garage door company.

It was proof.

Proof that I could create something from nothing.

Proof that I could build trust with strangers just by being me.

Proof that hustle, heart, and honesty would always open more doors than any fancy truck or title ever could.

That first job from Ashley and Dave?

It changed my life—not because of the money, but because they *saw* me.

They believed in a young man who didn't even believe fully in himself yet.

And that one belief created a ripple effect that still reaches me today.

Sometimes all it takes is one opportunity, one connection, one yes—to unlock the life you were meant to build.

In this chapter, I learned that when you serve with sincerity, the world shows up for you.

Clients become mentors.

Jobs become stepping stones.

Ugly trucks become painted symbols of transformation.

Entrepreneurship wasn't the goal. Growth was.

I didn't just build a business—I began rebuilding myself.

I wasn't chasing success anymore. I was creating value.

Responsible. Reliable. Rooted in something bigger than me.

And maybe most importantly...

I was learning to take care of something else—Gunner.

He kept me alive. He grounded me.

Because sometimes, the most unexpected companions show up to guide us back to ourselves.

The lesson I hope you take from this: You don't have to have it all figured out to get started. You just have to start.

Let's keep going.

— **Trapper**

CHAPTER 7

Sam

Back when I was strictly a party boy, I met Jasmine. Like me, all she was interested in was playing, drinking, and hooking up. We were good together. Then I started focusing on Gunner and The Garage Doctor, and we split on good terms. One night, she texted me. "I'm bringing a group of girls to the Donkey Den bar. You should come. I think you'll really hit it off with my friend, Samantha."

My roommate, Seth, and I got to the bar at about nine that night. Shortly after, Jasmine walked in, a line of four or five girls following. I was struck by the girl right behind her. Our eyes locked for just a moment. I turned to Seth and said, "I don't know who that is, but I'm going to marry that girl."

They came to our table. Jasmine introduced her. "Trapper, this is Sam."

We started talking and almost instantly dissolved into our own bubble, the rest of the room fading away. If I'd known I was going to marry her before we'd been introduced, that sense was only confirmed. Our connection was solid. I had no idea why or how, and didn't care. Sam was the one for me.

Like almost everyone I met for the first time, Sam wanted to know about my name. Was it a nickname? And, as always, I said, "No, it's my name. I can prove it."

I pulled out my driver's license and handed it to her.

She laughed," No way!"

"Yep - that's my real name. Crazy, huh?"

"No, not your name - we have the same birthday."

"No way!"

"Yes, I was born February 16, 1979. So I'm older - can you handle that?"
You bet I could.

We danced. I wanted to kiss her. We took a cab back to her house. Could I crash on her couch? Sure. Once inside, her friend, Ariana, stumbled to the couch and passed out. Her roommate, Shannon, climbed the stairs to her room, and I offered to sleep on the floor or get a cab back to my place.

"You can sleep with me," Sam said. "But nothing's going to happen."

"Okay," I said. "I don't want to hook up. I want to see you again."

We lay awake all night while I unpacked my baggage - all of it. If I had shame, I told her. If I'd screwed up, she knew about it. I wanted Sam for life. I wasn't about to keep anything from her. She was getting all of me: good, bad, and everything in between. She listened and didn't run. There could be no doubt in her mind that what she was getting with me was full honesty and utter transparency.

"I'm poor. I just started a company. I have no money."

She had graduated from the University of Colorado and had a job as a marketing director for a local company. Her parents were well off. Was I in her league? If not, I didn't care. I was in love and was prepared to step up to whatever level I needed to.

I had no idea what I was supposed to step up to. It might have been wise for me to ask, "Sam, what are your expectations of me? What do you want in life?"

But I didn't ask. Her expectations might have been so much simpler than I imagined. But all I knew was that her parents lived lavishly and her father was the most successful man I had ever met. I assumed she wanted to be on a par with her parents. I was sure I could work harder and strive more, reaching for that star, because I was determined to stay ahead of everyone else in every way possible, including financially. I was in a race, and I was resolute about winning. The Garage Doctor was going to do super well.

Now that Sam was in my life, I became the person who could achieve anything he set his mind to, but that person was also going to be super stressed in pursuit of his goals.

Sam and I became inseparable; she stayed at my place, or I went to hers. Then her roommate got ready to move, and Sam talked to her parents about buying a house or condo with their help. Sam asked me to come and look at the apartments downtown with her. If we were going to do this together, downtown wouldn't work for me. I had a dog and a truck, so I couldn't possibly park on a crowded city street.

"I know you want to live downtown," I said. "But I've got a big dog and a big truck. Why don't we look at buying a house?"

Her parents, Steve and Debbie, were not impressed - not with the idea of us buying a house, and not with me. I had horrible credit, and my company was brand new. Her father was particularly adamant that if we did this, I had to keep track of the time I put into fixing the house, and either Sam or the family could pay me for that. He wanted to ensure that, if and when we broke up, there would be no loose ends to tidy up. I'd only met Sam's parents twice, and while they'd been nice enough, they hadn't exactly embraced me. I hadn't gone to college, I was from Wyoming, I was obviously a redneck, and I drank a lot.

I took Sam to Casper to meet my parents, stopping at the Eastridge Mall when we arrived early. Wandering around the mall, we walked into a pet store displaying a Shih-Tzu litter. She fell in love with one of them, paid the several hundred dollars, and walked out with the little pup in her arms - and I was jealous! This little pup was going to demand too much of Sam's time! What about me?

And then I introduced Sam to my parents. "Are you Christian?" they asked.

"No, I'm Jewish."

It was all downhill from there. I should be with a good Christian girl, they said.

Really?

We walked away, and they didn't talk to me for at least half a year. I didn't care. Since living in Denver, I'd seen a lot more of life than the little world of

Casper, Wyoming, had to offer. I liked being exposed to different cultures, ideas, and ways of thinking. I was not about to go back to a narrow, blindered way of life.

Sam and I bought a house in early 2006. Once we moved in, her father, Steve, called me daily. "Hey, how's work going?"

Was he checking up on me?

Probably.

Sam's parents flew us to her godsister, Jessica's, wedding in Eastern Washington State. Jessica's father, Alan, a successful businessman, went all out on the reception. Sam's younger brother, Taylor, who is my age, kept pace with me at the open bar. We were throwing back utterly delicious shots. I liked them so much that I asked the bartender to give me a tray. She complied, and I walked around the room, balancing about 30 shot glasses and passing them out to the other guests.

I approached Alan with my tray. "Alan! You've got to have one of these."

"What is it?"

"I don't know, but it's free alcohol!"

"I know! I'm paying for it."

I turned to the room. "Drinks are on Alan!"

Steve was drinking, but he was also smoking a lot of weed. Great! Steve was a pothead. He and Debbie were also holding hands, giving off warm, sensual vibes. He didn't hesitate to tap her bottom or put his arms around her. Wonderful. Maybe we had something in common after all.

I believe Steve began to accept me to some degree, seeing that I genuinely loved Sam and was playful with her, yet also respectful.

Steve probably thought Sam and I would be together for a couple of years. Then she'd meet a nice Jewish boy and marry him. Maybe he would be a doctor, a lawyer, or a respectable businessman.

But Sam and I were saving money to go on a vacation to Cabo San Lucas. After we booked it, I called Debbie, Sam's mother. "Hey Debbie, I've been saving some money. Would it be cool with you if I proposed to Sam?"

"I love it!" she said. "You're awesome. Have you talked to Steve?"

"God, no!" I said."I wasn't going to ask Steve, so I called you. You talk to Steve."

"Do you have a ring?" she asked.

"Yes." I'd bought a ring from Jared's for four hundred dollars, and even that had taken me four months to pay off.

Soon after that conversation, I started getting calls from Sam's younger brother, Taylor, from Sam's best friend and other friends. Great - if all these people knew, then Steve probably did too. Calling him no longer felt so scary.

Sam was going out on a girls' night. I watched her drive away with her friends and took a deep breath. Then another. I steadied my hands. Okay - ready. I dialed Steve's number.

"Hey, Steve! How's it going?"

"Yeah - what's up?"

"Have you got a few minutes?"

"Yeah - what've you got?"

"Well, Sam and I are going to Cabo this weekend."

"Yeah - that should be fun for you guys. You good? You need any money?"

"No, I don't need any money. I'm going to ask Sam to marry me."

The line went dead. Oh fuck. That's not good. What just happened? He didn't even say anything! He just hung up!

Breathing hard, I called Taylor, Sam's younger brother. No answer.

I called Debbie. "Debbie - Steve just hung up on me!"

"I know. He just stormed out of the house."

"What the fuck!"

"What did you say to him?"

"I told him I'm going to ask Sam to marry me - and he hung up!"

"I don't know what to tell you," she said. "He just left. He's gone."

I paced the room. What was going on? Was he going to fly out here? I called Seth. I called Josh. I called everyone I knew. But what could they do besides listen to me curse over the phone? This was not good. I called Steve's friend, Alan. No answer. I sat in my office, ready to vomit.

At midnight, my phone rang.

"Hey, Steve," I said. "I'm sorry. Did I catch you off guard?"

"I really don't want you to marry Sam," he said.

"Why not? I really love her."

"I know. I see it. But you have to understand. Sam's my only daughter. I want her to be happy and I want her to live a good life."

"Me too," I said. "I know you don't know me very well, but that's important to me too."

"Are you going to raise your kids Jewish?" he asked.

"I don't know," I said. "If that's important to Samantha, we can talk about it, but I'm not going to lie to you."

A pause, and then, "Would you consider learning more about our religion?"

"Sure, I'll educate myself, and I'll respect that. But I can't promise that we're going to raise our kids Jewish. I don't even know if Sam wants to do that."

"When she has a baby, it's going to be Jewish," he said. "When a child is born to a Jewish mother, they're Jewish."

"Okay," I said.

"What's your credit score?" he asked.

"My what?"

"What is your credit score?"

"I don't know. What is that?"

"You need to know what it is," Steve said. "Your whole life is going to be dictated by it."

"If you want to teach me what it is, I'll learn," I said.

"Do you have any credit cards?" he asked.

"Oh yeah, I've got a few."

"That can't be good."

"No, it isn't. I've got a ton of debt."

Another pause. "Tell you what," he said. "When are you going to propose?"

"This weekend."

"I think you should wait. Wait until you get your credit score up and until you get more of a grip on what you want to do with your life."

"But I know what I want to do with my life," I said.

"And what do you want to do?"

"I want to marry your daughter, Steve."

Perhaps I should have had the presence of mind to say, "I want to marry Sam and create the best life that we can, and that includes a lot of things." But I was young and not thinking ahead to a house and a big, thriving business. However, I didn't say that I wanted to be a successful entrepreneur, nor did I want my business to grow beyond just a one-man operation.

I could have said, "I want to marry Sam, build a business, and create a legacy. I want a family with Sam – we both share that desire. I want to travel, and everything I want to do, I want to do with Sam."

I said all those things, in retrospect, in my own head.

Steve and I kept discussing religion and politics until I saw Sam driving up at about 2 a.m. "Steve," I said. Sam just pulled up. I've got to get off the phone, but I'm going to ask Sam to marry me, and she's going to say yes. I'm not actually asking for your blessing at this point, I'm just telling you that I'm going to marry your daughter, and I'm going to give her my best."

The next day, we packed and flew to Cabo, where we stayed at the Marina Fiesta. Everywhere we went, out on the pier, to the local taco stand, into the town - I carried the ring in my pocket, constantly reaching in, touching the small jeweler's box, making sure it was there - waiting for the moment when my stomach wasn't doing flip-flops.

One day near sunset, we were walking on the beach, talking about our dreams. She was looking out at the ocean while I stood behind her, my arms wrapped around her waist. I dropped my arms and got down on one knee. She turned. "Will you marry me?" I asked.

Her mouth opened. "What?"

Wait, she was supposed to jump into my arms and shout "Yes!"

"If you're not ready, it's okay," I muttered.

"No," she said. "Did you just ask me to marry you?"

"Yes. I have a ring and everything."

"Yes," she said, and then, "Did you talk to my dad?"

"I tried," I said. "That's why I was on the phone the other night."

It didn't matter what he'd said. Sam had said yes. I slipped the ring on her finger, and my new life began.

Perspective Shift

There are moments in life where everything changes—not in chaos, but in clarity.

Meeting Sam was one of those moments.

From the second our eyes locked at the Donkey Den, something in me knew.

Not the surface-level kind of knowing.

Not the infatuation or the attraction or the "wow, she's hot."

This was soul-deep. She was my person.

It's wild to think I told Seth I was going to marry her before I even knew her name.

But that's what happens when your heart recognizes home.

What I didn't realize then was that love like that doesn't just challenge you—it shapes you.

Being with Sam didn't make me perfect.

It made me want to grow—to become the kind of man worthy of that kind of love.

And in trying to be "enough," I pushed myself harder than ever before.

That's the lesson here:

Sometimes love doesn't show up wrapped in a fairy tale.

Sometimes, it shows up with questions, culture clashes, family pressure, and the weight of your own insecurities...

But if you're willing—really willing—to be seen, to stay honest, and to choose your person anyway, that's where real connection lives.

I didn't have a six-figure bank account or a credit score that impressed anybody.

But I had a dream, a work ethic, and a heart full of commitment.

Sam didn't fall in love with my resume.

She fell in love with my realness.

And because of that, I stopped trying to be someone else's version of successful.

I decided I would build our life from the inside out—with love, truth, and relentless effort.

This chapter was the start of something much bigger than a love story.

Love will test you.

It'll ask you who you are and who you're willing to become.

Say yes.

Every time.

Let's keep going. The story's just getting started.

—Trapper

CHAPTER 8

Getting Help

Back home from Cabo, our lives followed the trajectory of most newly engaged couples. Sam's mom, Debbie, was excited; her dad, Steve, was less so, but gracious and warm because he knew we were getting married, and the wisest attitude was to embrace the fact. Sam and Debbie dove headfirst into wedding plans while I continued to work hard at growing my business. Steve, who also owned a business, began to take an interest in what I was doing, and we continued to talk every day. Week by week, and step by step, we became friends.

We talked about art, watches, and business, and he taught me so much. He told me about credit scores and how important they were if I wanted to afford nice things in life. From him, I learned that when you are successful, you don't have to flaunt it. He taught me how to be a good person.

Sam and I worked and socialized with friends. I did "stuff" around the house, like fixing a leaky faucet and mowing the lawn. We were turning our house into a home, and my life was beginning to feel "normal." The fact that I had a fine house in a nice neighborhood didn't feel strange. It may not have been the lifestyle I'd grown up with, but I'd had high expectations of myself for as far back as I could remember. I knew I deserved this—and more. I was going to be a married man, and we were going to have a family. I had a vision of what that should look like, mainly the complete opposite of how I had grown up.

I did have insecurities, and they centered around Sam. Why was she with me? Sam had gone to college. I had not. She was four years older. She was smart and beautiful. What did she see in me? I couldn't tell myself I was a successful entrepreneur because I didn't even know what that was. Having created a job for myself, I was simply self-employed.

The only answer to my questions was to create something so valuable that she wouldn't want to leave. After all, at this point, what did I have to offer this beautiful, smart, young woman?

Underlying my stress and insecurity was a smoldering hotbed of anger, not directed at Sam but myself. I wasn't drinking much anymore, but when I did, I drank a lot, and when I was drunk, I turned every dark emotion I experienced inward. I didn't give myself compassion or kindness - just the opposite.

Like most young people, when I fell in love with Sam, I sold her the best version of myself and the me I hoped I would one day be. Today, I know who I am. I don't feel the need to sell myself at all. I know my value lies in what I give and the excellence I strive for every day. If people don't respect that or reciprocate, they're not my people.

But that's now.

When I was twenty-two and freshly engaged and in love, I did not recognize my value, and the dark side lay close to the surface. Maybe I should have been taking my Xanax, but the dose I'd been prescribed was high enough that it just knocked me out within ten minutes, and I had no desire to spend half my life sleepwalking. And I didn't see Xanax as a long-term solution.

Not long after returning from Cabo, my mother called. I was drinking, and her words triggered feelings I couldn't control. Even though I was sending my parents five hundred dollars a month to help them get by, she still attacked me with the same harangue I listened to each time she called. She told me how lazy my dad was, implying I was just like him. She never acknowledged how hard I was working or how I was trying to better myself. I wanted that acknowledgement badly. I was always helping people. I'd help someone change a tire at the side of the road. I'd shovel the walk for the old couple down the block. If a dog was lost, I'd pick him up. I was on a mission to be acknowledged for being a good person. I didn't have to send money to my parents, but I did it because they were struggling, and it was the right thing to do - and still, my mother refused to acknowledge me.

"Lazy" was my biggest trigger word, because it was so palpably untrue. All she had to do to fuel the rage inside me was to say that word. And then, instead of asking how I was doing, she would give me an interminable rundown of the misery of her life.

"Fuck!" I thought, listening to her. "Ask me how I am! And if you don't like your life, you're an adult. Make a change! Do something that positively impacts your life!"

I hung up, the angry fire in me erupting like a long-dormant volcano. I grabbed a baseball bat, tore into the backyard to the big old cottonwood tree in the corner, and started beating at the trunk, sweat and tears dripping off me. I beat and beat, my teeth locked, screams inside me.

I finally collapsed, my arms limp, my body spent, I hunkered down on the ground, leaning back against the cottonwood, tears streaming down my face, my rage simmering now on low. Gunner and Sophie, the two dogs, ran out, sniffing at my hands, Gunner licking the tears off my cheek.

Sam followed behind the dogs, hesitant and unsure of what to expect next. This wasn't the Trapper she knew. I saw the fear in her, not fear of me, but for me.

She came closer. "Trapper, we need to get this under control. I don't want to be a part of this, and I don't think you do either."

No, of course she didn't want to be part of it. If I didn't take care of the demons, I might lose her. Of course, I needed to heal for myself, but in that moment, I vowed to do whatever it would take to keep her.

Sam was the first person to acknowledge me for who I was. She saw me. Sitting up against the tree at that moment, I was at the bottom of my personal pit. And still, she hadn't turned and walked away — she had come to me with an offer to help.

With her encouragement, I acknowledged that I had problems and reached out for help. I made an appointment with Dr Compton, my primary care physician.

Sitting in her office, I said, "I don't know if you're the right person for this, but I think I need a mental evaluation. I'm not in a good place. I'm getting married and I have anxiety attacks." I explained how angry I would get and how I would explode.

"I can help with medication," she said. "But you have to be evaluated by a psychological professional."

She recommended Tamara Hughes, who became my go-to therapist. During my first visit, she struck me as kind, caring, and competent. For the first few months, we scheduled my sessions three days a week. It was expensive, but I saw it as a tremendously worthwhile investment in myself. I discovered quickly that therapy is far less about what the therapist does for you than it is about a safe place where you can talk with complete candor and vulnerability. When you're in a therapist's office, you're in a place where no one judges you and no one has a vested interest in who you are, what you do, or what you say. I found my sessions profoundly freeing. With every visit, I saw a bigger payoff for my investment.

Talking to someone with no walls between us was a remarkable experience. I told myself I should be this open with Sam. I should be able to talk to her about anything, but I was still young and immature at twenty-two. I wasn't about to share with her the dysfunction and trauma of my childhood and youth. I thought I'd told her all the important stuff that first night we were together, but tell her I was this messed up? No way! Somewhere in the back of my mind, I thought, *Maybe with a safe place to talk about all this stuff, I can correct it, and Sam doesn't have to know about it.*

I was naive. I didn't know how severely those early wounds were affecting my life every day. As my therapy progressed, I realized I had a lot to unpack. Keeping all that baggage packed away was probably not going to be an option. My issues would continue to spill over into my relationship with Sam.

I had an inkling then that I didn't fully grasp until much later, about how we operate in the world. We go to work and put our best efforts into doing a good job. We go to church or to a sports team we belong to, or possibly a club, and we give our best. But then we go home to our family, and they get what's left over. Those leftovers are sometimes frustrations, complaints, and just plain weariness.

I came to understand that's completely backwards. I was giving a hundred percent to people at work who really didn't care about me, and then came home and gave my family sixty percent or maybe only twenty. I should be giving my family a hundred percent. With that foundation of love and support to build on, I could easily give a hundred percent to work and everyone else. And even if my workday was awful, I'd still be left with a hundred percent to give back to my family.

I wish I had learned that earlier. I wish I'd known about the wedding, which was now looming, with planning and preparations taking up most of our time.

Perspective Shift

This was the chapter in which I finally turned the mirror inward, not to judge myself but to understand myself.

Up until this point, I'd built a lot.

A business. A home. A relationship.

But I hadn't built any real tools for healing.

I was still running from the shadows I carried as a kid—the ones I thought I could outwork, outperform, or just ignore until they disappeared.

You can't outrun what's inside you.

Not with success. Not with relationships. Not even with love.

At some point, your pain will demand to be heard.

And if you don't listen, it will roar.

That day in the backyard with a bat and a heart full of rage...

That was the moment I knew I had to stop surviving and start healing.

Not just for Sam.

Not just for the future I wanted.

But for me.

And the biggest lesson I learned?

Getting help doesn't mean you're broken.

It means you've stopped pretending you can carry it all alone.

Therapy wasn't weakness.

It was my first real act of strength.

If you're reading this and carrying pain from your past.

You don't have to.

Your healing can begin the moment you stop hiding it.

Let someone help you unpack.

You're not too far gone. You're not too complicated. You're not unworthy.

You're human.

Let's keep going.

—**Trapper**

CHAPTER 9

The Wedding

The days leading up to the wedding intensified as the date grew closer. But I was one of those grooms who said, "Just tell me what to wear and what time to show up."

Sam's mom, Debbie, and Debbie's best friend, Bunny, were swimming in the deep end. How big was this thing going to be? And how much would it cost? Sam and I didn't have any money to spare. Steve was there for us, "I'm going to pay for the wedding," he said.

We were pretty good friends by then. "Well yeah, you said there were going to be about two hundred people, so I'm not going to be paying for that shit."

We still talked every day. He liked to check in to see how my business was doing. And then we found we had something in common. I didn't have much money, but I had taken a liking to wrist watches. They weren't expensive, and I started buying them when I had a bit of extra coin. Steve was delighted when I told him because he loved timepieces, and from then on, we talked about watches at least once or twice a week.

Steve warmed to me more quickly than either of us expected because he had also struggled when he was young. Now he had a big house on several acres in Redmond near Seattle, a landscaper who kept his lawn looking like a putting green, and a Mercedes convertible. However, he drove an old Jeep Grand Cherokee to work during meetings with his team. He was not the kind of guy to brag and show off his wealth.

We flew to Seattle a couple of times during the wedding's planning stage. Debbie and Sam discussed dresses and decorations, while Steve and I chatted about every subject we were interested in. As we grew closer, I recognized him as a pretty special man, so generous that he would literally give you the shirt off his back if you needed it.

I had to get involved in some of the arrangements, like the guest list. I couldn't top twenty people, including my parents, my sister's family, and my friends. Sam's side looked like the roll call at a White House state dinner. I'd been to a few weddings of former classmates, and they pretty much followed the format of a backyard barbecue with cases of Bud Light in a bucket of ice. It looked like Steve and Debbie were aiming to top Jessica's wedding, which had blown me away.

Our date was October 6, 2007, and Sam and Debbie settled on The Palace Ballroom in downtown Seattle, a venue well-known for its grand weddings and exceptional catered food. My groomsmen were Jared, Seth, Josh, and Taylor, Sam's brother. They were all my "best men," but technically, Jared was responsible for not losing the ring.

The morning of the big day, Sam and I dressed in our best duds, me in a tux, and Sam in a cloud of white, looking more beautiful than I had ever seen her - and she was gorgeous every time I laid eyes on her. Her father had the day planned, starting with the arrival of a classic Rolls-Royce. Trailed by a crew of photographers and videographers, we visited all the most photogenic locations in Seattle, including the infamous Gum Wall, the Space Needle, and Pike Place Market. Because it was just the two of us and the crew, we had time to soak up the experience of living a day focused totally on our joy.

With photos completed, we pulled up in front of the Palace Ballroom. The crew mic'd us up for the audio portion of our video. A Rabbi performed the ceremony, I broke the glass with my foot, and we were married. While I basked in the miracle of having a wife, we had to leave the ballroom briefly while the staff changed the room from ceremonial configuration to reception hall.

My buddies headed to the bar while Sam and I retired to the small suite reserved for us. We relaxed on the couch, grinning hugely at each other.

"It's kind of hot in here," Sam said.

"It sure is," I agreed.

"Do you want to kill some time?" she asked.

My smile got bigger. "Sure. Let's kill some time."

Sweet, delightful, and sensuous play time! Sam had just finished taking care of me when I noticed the door starting to open.

"Hold on!" I yelled. "Give us a minute!"

Frantically, Sam and I straightened our clothing. Just in time, because the door swung open and Sam's father walked in. Did he notice our awkward smiles and slightly disheveled hair?

Probably.

Steve sat beside me on the couch, put his hand on my leg, and said, "You guys are really doing great."

Meanwhile, my inside voice was saying, *Oh my god! Thirty seconds sooner and you would have had a different experience, Steve.*

He hugged us both, kissed Sam on the cheek, and left. The door closed behind him, we looked at each other, and started laughing so hard, we almost fell on the floor.

Then we heard the knock on the door, alerting us that the hall was ready. We entered the reception holding hands."Let's give a big welcome to Trapper and Samantha Searles! Mr. and Mrs. Searles!" I heard the wild applause, smiled, walked to the head table, and stared in amazement at the most spectacular wedding cake I'd ever seen adorned by a topper that even included marzipan figures of our dogs.

Just as we were sitting down, the wedding planner approached us. "Hey," she said. "We're going to be editing the video and the sound, but you should know that you were on full audio, and the whole crew heard you during - um - intermission. It was all recorded. Do you want us to edit that out?"

Sam and I looked at each other, grinning. "Fuck no! Leave it in there."

We ended up with two videos, one of them just for us.

The rest of the evening spun so quickly that it was impossible to absorb it all. It was the first time my parents had seen my sister since she'd moved out of their house years before. Their reunion wasn't warm, but it was cordial, and I was happy about that. Our playlist was killer. The food was beyond delicious - or so I heard. I was endlessly shaking hands and saying, "Hi, I'm Trapper. So nice to meet you."

And then there was a trip to the hospital. Jared, who had to be careful with food because he had a narrow esophagus, got a piece of steak stuck in his throat. Seth couldn't dislodge it with a Heimlich maneuver, so eight or nine of us, including Sam in her wedding dress, piled into a friend's Toyota Camry and sped to the hospital.

Back at the Palace Ballroom, the guests kept dancing and drinking, unaware of the drama occurring a few blocks away. When we got back, the party was still going strong. When it finally began to wind down, we managed to quell some of our hunger pangs with mini pastries from the donut bar.

When the night was finally over, we headed back to the hotel, fell into bed exhausted, and went to sleep. We took our honeymoon trip a few months later. For now, it was time to get to work. But we did hear from our friends for months and even years afterwards, that ours was the most bad-ass wedding they'd ever attended.

Perspective Shift

This chapter might read like the best rom-com of my life—because it was.

Wild, sweet, hilarious, emotional… and somehow, perfectly us.

But here's what really sticks with me when I look back:

A wedding is one day.

A marriage is every day after that.

It's easy to get caught up in the details—guest lists, seating charts, whether the cake has buttercream or fondant. But what matters most can't be scripted or styled. It's those in-between moments—standing on a beach together, laughing through nerves, kissing on a couch when the world goes quiet. That's where the magic lives.

I wasn't just saying "I do" to a woman.

I was saying, "I will."

I will show up when I'm tired.

I will try again when I fail.

I will become the man our life together deserves.

And let me tell you something real…

The day was beautiful. It was grand. It was unforgettable.

But my favorite moment?

It was the laughter after almost getting caught with our pants down—literally.

That right there—that's us. Messy. Joyful. Honest. Real.

So if you're walking into your own big moment, or dreaming of it someday, remember this:

The best weddings reflect who you are.

The best marriages are built on who you choose to become—together.

Let the playlist bang. Let the memories roll.

And then get ready—because the real adventure starts after the music fades.

Let's keep going.

—Trapper

CHAPTER 10

Another Heartbreak

I thought marriage would make me different, or make us different. At the very least, there would be tax benefits. But the world didn't stop spinning. Sam and I continued to have fun. We worked, played, and went out with our friends. Nothing changed dramatically.

I remember how our house became a home. We had Gunner and Sophie running around our big grassed backyard. I'd be working in the shop on all kinds of projects. Samantha would be out on the deck enjoying the sun or keeping me company. We remodeled the bathroom and did many house projects ourselves, the way I'd envisioned most young couples. We had a four-wheeler, a side-by-side, and a camper that filled most of our weekends. We loved hitting the mountain with friends. The work was exciting, and the money was coming in. I even bought a new truck. Sam and I had fun.

Sam traveled for work occasionally, and she was in Dallas in 2010, the week before we had booked airline tickets to fly to Seattle to attend her father, Steve's, sixtieth birthday celebration at Lake Chelan. Sam adored her father. When she had problems or questions, or if she just wanted to talk, she'd turn to Steve. I did too. We continued to talk almost every day. He had become one of my best friends, mentor, advisor, and in many ways, a father figure I'd always needed.

Jessica, Sam's best friend, called me from Los Angeles. "Trapper, Steve passed away. You need to call Sam."

I hung up. Steve? Gone? Impossible! He wasn't sick. I'd just talked to him the day before. He was fine. He had no medical conditions. He couldn't be gone!

In a daze, I called Sam. I knew then that I'd only been playing at being a husband. It was time to step up. I had to be there for Sam because that was what being a husband was about - being the person Sam could lean on in times of trauma.

Sam answered the phone with her peppy, energetic "Hi!"

"Hey, babe," I said. "You need to get out to Seattle as soon as you can," I said, as my heart sank.

"What's wrong?"

"Your dad has died." All the breath left my body with those words. When I said that to them, I knew it was true. Steve was gone. Steve: the foundation of the family, the glue that held everyone together. He'd always had a knack for gathering friends and family around him, creating a space that declared, "We are a family!"

Sam caught the next available flight from Dallas to Seattle, and I flew to Seattle to meet her. The day Steve died, everything changed. The bottom dropped out of Sam's world.

Her mother, Debbie, her brother, Taylor, and Sam clung to each other in their grief. I was helpless to stop their tears while suppressing my own. What right did I have to weep for a man I'd loved for only four years when they had a lifetime of memories to grieve?

I put myself to work as the airport shuttle driver, picking up family flying in from New York, Chicago, and Oregon. I was determined to be the rock that could be relied on to handle anything that might come up.

The hard lump in my chest continued to build. Friends and family gathered, asking Sam, Debbie, and Taylor how they were doing. Could they do anything to help? No one asked me. Was I selfish for wanting them to? Why couldn't anyone see how much Steve had meant to me?

Through those muddled days of people coming and going, through evenings of tears and hugs, I would find moments to duck away and locate a space, just to feel the pain in my heart. But I never dug into it deeply. I didn't know how brokenhearted I was over my loss, or how big a space he had filled in my life. Debbie told me Steve had died of a ruptured aortic valve. He'd called his best friend, Alan Klein, when he was feeling strange, telling him his leg felt oddly heavy. Alan told him to call an ambulance. Steve had internal bleeding, and by the time the ambulance arrived at Washington Medical Center, the bleeding had reached his brain. He died quickly.

The days after Steve's death were a blur. While people, probably Debbie, handled the arrangements, I hovered in the background. At least two hundred people came to the synagogue for the service, so many that some had to watch it on monitors outside the main room. He wasn't just the foundation of his family, but also his community.

I stayed outside, pacing small circles in front of the closed doors. I couldn't walk into that room. My sadness was threatening to overwhelm me, and I didn't want to know what was over the edge if I tipped and lost control.

When the doors finally opened, Steve's best friends, Alan, Murray, and Tom, walked out and came toward me. I was trying to keep it together, but probably failing. Tom put his arm around my shoulders. "Trapper," he said. "He really loved you. Remember when he hung up on you when you asked to marry Sam?"

I nodded, tears leaking from my eyes.

"Well, he called all of us and asked what we thought about you. We all gave him our blessings."

They couldn't have said anything better to soothe the ache in my chest. And at the same time, nothing they said could have been more guaranteed to make me cry and miss him so much. They had just lost their best friend, yet they had taken the time to care about me. My gratitude brought more tears.

At the cemetery, we held another small ceremony, exclusive to the family. We carried the casket to the grave and slowly lowered it. Before covering it with dirt, people were invited to throw items into the grave that reminded them of Steve. An awful lot of weed landed on the casket that day.

Debbie, Taylor, Sam, and I were the last to leave. If not for the heavy rock in my chest, I could have floated away. I was empty, light as air. All I felt was the emptiness of loss and the heavy weight of grief that kept me on the earth.

Less than a week later, Steve's mother, who suffered from dementia, also died. We stayed for another funeral before flying home.

It's only in looking back that I realize how dramatically Steve's death affected our lives. Sam's big smile and laughter vanished. She walked through the house like a shadow. She wanted to talk to someone about her pain, but her confidant was gone. Not knowing what to do, I retreated into myself. I understood the emptiness Sam was feeling, because I felt it too, but I also felt guilty about feeling so hurt and upset by Steve's death. I had no right to feel this sad. My wife had lost her dad. I should step up. But what did stepping up mean in this situation?

Looking back, I wish we had talked about our loss. Instead of talking to each other, I saw a therapist while Sam held her feelings inside.

We had other problems that were exacerbating the increasing rift in our marriage. We'd been trying to get pregnant for a few months, and we were coming up empty.

Perspective Shift

Losing Steve shook the foundation of our world. Not just Sam's world—ours. He wasn't just my father-in-law. He was my mentor, friend, and anchor when I felt adrift. And suddenly, he was gone. No warning. No goodbye. Just... gone.

We were both hurting. Both drowning. And we never looked each other in the eye to say, "Hey, I miss him too. I don't know how to live without him either."

I thought I didn't have the right to grieve—because he wasn't my dad.

But here's the truth I know now:

Grief doesn't need permission.

It just needs a place to breathe.

Steve's death created a silence in our home that neither of us knew how to fill. And without words, pain built walls between us. We were both walking ghosts, under the same roof, but so alone.

If I could go back, I'd sit with Sam and say,

"We don't have to be okay. We just have to be here—for each other."

And I'd tell myself:

You don't have to carry it all alone.

You're allowed to grieve.

You're allowed to fall apart.

You just don't have to do it in silence.

This chapter taught me something I'll never forget:

Real strength isn't silence.

Real strength is connection, even in pain.

If you've lost someone, don't wait to process the grief. Don't fake your way through it. Find the people who see you, and let them in.

Even now, I still miss Steve. And that ache?

It reminds me I had the gift of being loved deeply—and of loving him right back.

Let's keep going.

—**Trapper**

CHAPTER 11

Jaiden

Sam and I had always wanted a family. All our friends were well on their way. We attended numerous celebration parties - yay, we're pregnant! We were thrilled for them, anticipating the day we would make the happy announcement.

We kept trying, but after about eighteen months, we were feeling frustrated. Our friends weren't just celebrating pregnancies, they were showing off their babies. Their carefree joy became downright annoying. Sam's mom, Debbie, would ask when we'd make her a grandmother. My parents demanded to know when we were going to start a family. We took our frustration out on each other, fighting over nothing, and blaming each other for everything that went wrong.

Our parents thought that if you were with the right person, you should be able to procreate. It was natural. They had done it. Maybe there was something wrong in our relationship. I began to think that maybe there was. Maybe we shouldn't be together. A slow anger started simmering inside me.

One day, we were at a dinner party with friends. We were all drinking wine, except Tara. She and Chris, her husband, already had a son. "Hey, Tara," I said. "Why aren't you drinking? Are you pregnant again?"

She gave me the biggest smile. "Yes, with twins!"

My simmering anger rose to a boil. I turned to Sam, "Let's fucking go!"

Sam knew better than to argue. I grabbed her hand and we left.

Babies and pregnant women were everywhere. If I walked along the street, I couldn't go a block or two without seeing moms pushing strollers or holding a baby in a Snugli close to their chest. And no matter how much Sam and I wanted that, we weren't getting it. I felt like a failure. I'm sure Sam felt the same. We continued to question whether we should even stay together.

Then in 2011, Sam's mom announced that she was taking the family to Hawaii, maybe to turn the page on Steve's death and give everyone a reason to have fun. Debbie, Taylor, his wife, Robin, Sam and I boarded a flight out of Seattle, landing in Honolulu to a warm breeze ruffling the tops of the tall palms.

I should have been happy, but I couldn't get there. I'd left the mainland behind, but not my anger or frustration. I hated the world. I had to blame someone for Steve's death, and raging at the world was better than tearing at my own heart, although I did that too.

If Steve were still alive, I'd have someone to talk to about all these feelings - but he wasn't there. How dare he die!

We were staying at a luxurious oceanfront resort. When we weren't sitting on the beach, we toured the area. We visited Pearl Harbor and toured the USS Arizona, aiming to make a memorable trip. I dragged my sorry ass along. I didn't want to be around the family, not even Sam. I'm pretty sure she didn't want to be around me either.

One day, Sam and I exploded at each other, hurling words we would one day regret. I channeled my mother's voice, spewing out words I'd grown up with, knowing they would wound deeply, and not caring. "This is bullshit! What are we doing? We can't even have a kid! "I'm fucking leaving!"

Years of emotions flooded me, threatening to drown me. I'd fallen in love with Sam at first sight, and then I'd met her family - aunts, uncles, cousins - and I'd known, "This is what a family is supposed to be like." I experienced a love I'd always craved. Everyone loved and supported each other. And then Steve died, and it all fell apart. I lost a spark of life. My friend Seth's dad had been significant when I was growing up, but then Steve stepped right into my heart. I learned more from him in four years than I'd learned from anyone else to that point. If Steve was gone, what was the point of continuing as if life was back to normal? It wasn't! It never would be!

Honestly? With Steve gone, life sucked.

The family didn't feel like a family anymore. Sam and I couldn't have a baby. Everybody around us was having a baby. Everyone else had a great family. Everyone else was in love. We were shit compared to them. In the game of life, we were losing.

Furious, I stuffed all my belongings into my suitcase and half-ran, half-walked to the top level of the parkade to get into the Jeep Grand Cherokee we'd rented. Sam ran after me, and Debbie and Taylor trailed behind. I lost my grip on the suitcase, dropping it on the cement. I didn't even stop to pick it up, tore upon the driver's side door, got in, slammed the door, and pulled out, tires screeching, running over the suitcase - and still not giving a damn.

I ripped down the street, pulling over when my heartbeat began to feel close to normal. I put my head down on the steering wheel and sobbed. I'd had the perfect life, and now it was falling apart - and all I could do was scream my anger.

I finally drove back to the hotel. Sam climbed into the jeep.

"Maybe this wasn't meant to be. Maybe we have to rethink our life together." I don't know who said those words. Probably both of us. For sure, divorce was on the table. But deep inside, I know I wanted to be married to Sam. I believe Sam felt the same way. But divorce just looked like the easy way out. If we stayed together, we had to do some heavy work.

We flew back home at the end of our week in Hawaii and threw ourselves into work. Garage Doctor was thriving, absorbing my attention all day, every day. Sam was just as busy building her career. And maybe because we were so wrapped up in doing what we loved, life smoothed itself out. It wasn't perfect, but it felt workable. Maybe we should keep trying for a baby.

With Debbie's help, we started in vitro fertilization treatments. It wasn't easy. Sam had to take hormones that swung her moods from high to low. The expense was huge. After a third failure, Debbie, Sam, and I met with the doctor, his Porsche parked in front of the office. "I think we're getting close," he said. "Maybe one more time."

I lost it. "What the fuck do you mean one more time? This is fifteen thousand dollars a try! We're making your car payments. By the time we're done with this, half of your car will be paid off! This is not moving my family forward!"

I added the doctor to the list of people, systems, and institutions that were out to get me. He'd already told us there was a problem with Sam's eggs - and now this. I was ready to give up. Nothing was working. What was wrong with us?

All I wanted was to be a dad. I was so furious now, I couldn't even be around my friends for fear of exploding.

Not long after that, my sister, Amber, called and said, "You know, we have friends who adopted. Just because you can't have a baby of your own, doesn't mean you're not meant to have a family. Maybe you're just meant to take a different path."

Maybe.

Shortly after that, we had lunch with our friends, Todd and Kristen, who had adopted a baby. And that sealed it. Okay, we were going to adopt. That's what we were meant to do. After all our arguments about not being meant to be together, we'd realized that yes, we were meant for each other. We just had to figure it out.

Then, Sam discovered that, through her company's insurance, she was entitled to a $10,000 adoption credit. Okay, that was a sign!

We started calling adoption agencies - fifteen in Colorado, and all of them religion-based. Because Sam was Jewish and I was unaffiliated and not much of a believer, we weren't qualified. No one would work with us.

Another dead end!

I was geared up for another meltdown when Sam heard about a different adoption agency called Creative Adoptions that had no restrictions on who you were or what you believed. You could be single, married, gay - it was all okay as long as you were ready to give a child a loving home. We started the process that included a home visit with a social worker and a look at our financial statements, which were looking very good.

The best part was creating an "About Us" book. We pulled out photos of us camping, playing outdoors, hugging, and just being together. We wrote about who we were and what we loved. We talked about food and travel - and somewhere in that process, we re-discovered what we valued in each other and why we were together. Yes, we were good together, and yes we could give a child a beautiful, loving home.

We submitted our book to the agency and prepared to wait. I was working on a client's garage in Aurora, an eastern suburb of Denver, when Sam called. "Trapper, I'm pregnant."

"What?"

Oh yes! Oh no! Wonderful, but she had to see a doctor right away. We knew she'd need hormones and other medical care immediately.

"I'm heading over to the doctor's office right away," she said. "I just found out. I missed my period a few days ago."

I dropped everything, told my customer I'd be back later, left my gear behind, and sped to the clinic. I ran to the reception desk. "Where's my wife?" I asked, followed her directions, and burst into her room. She was talking to her mom on the phone, tears pouring down her face.

She looked up at me. "I had a miscarriage," she said.

Sam was broken. I think we both were. Sam handed me the phone, damp from her tears. "Debbie, you should come out here," I said.

We pulled ourselves together and left the doctor's office. We were just stepping out on the sidewalk when Sam's phone rang. "Hello."

There was a pause. I watched Sam's mouth open and form a perfectly round "O". She looked at me, her eyes wide.

"What?"

"A mom just picked our book."

"What?"

Misery and deep sadness - and then suddenly, a fireworks of excitement! We'd been chosen! We were going to have a baby!

Sam and I grinned at each other like idiots.

I called Debbie. "Debbie. We're going to have a baby. We've been picked!"

We drove straight to the adoption agency, where they walked us carefully and clearly through the process. They set up a meeting with the mom-to-be. Stephanie was sixteen, just going into her second trimester. She was tiny, maybe a hundred pounds. Her mother, Kamilla, was there to support her. The best part? She said, "I'm so excited to have your baby." In her words, it was always "your baby" - never hers. "I was meant to be pregnant for someone else," she said.

The agency had warned us about the possibility that the mother might change her mind when the baby was born and placed in her arms. This happened frequently enough that they wanted us to be prepared "just in case." They told us not to decorate the baby's room—"just in case."

We were still on a roller-coaster ride.

Stephanie told us, "I loved your book. Trapper reminded me of my dad. I just felt you were the right people to raise this baby." She told us the baby's father was African American from St. Louis and wasn't in a good place to raise a child. Her own father had urged her to have an abortion.

Sam and Stephanie bonded quickly. Sam attended all of Stephanie's doctor's appointments. The pregnancy was progressing well, but as the time grew closer, our nerves started stretching thin. What if Stephanie changed her mind? What would happen when Stephanie held her baby for the first time? Hardly a day went by that we didn't walk by our empty bedroom, imagining its walls painted a buttery yellow, a pastel rainbow, or butterflies, and a crib with a pretty hummingbird mobile to catch the baby's eyes.

Even if all went well and we brought the baby home, Stephanie had ninety days to change her mind. It made sense, logical, and fair, but our hearts were far from it. Our moods swung from as high as the sky to as low as the cellar.

Stephanie gave us no cause to worry. "I'm not changing my mind," she said. "This is your baby." We painted the room, crossing our fingers we weren't jinxing it.

Stephanie's mother called us when her daughter went into labor on April 25, 2012. I believe it was about noon. Sam and I rushed to the hospital, and then we waited. Neither of us was allowed into the room, so we waited, paced, and drank coffee - so many cups of coffee. The hours ticked by. I finally sank to the floor outside the door to Stephanie's room. I closed my eyes, trying to imagine what was happening in there, and then we heard a tiny baby's first cry. I got to my feet; Sam got up from the chair. With tears in our eyes, we hugged, both of us thinking, "If she's holding her baby right now, there's no way she's going to give her to us."

We had to wait while they cleaned, weighed her, and did whatever doctors and nurses did with newborns. My fear skyrocketed. I called all my best friends. "What if she wants to keep the baby?" I don't remember one word they said back to me.

Finally, the nurse opened the door. "You can come in now." And there was Jaiden. The nurse placed this tiny, perfect little girl in Sam's arms, and of course, Sam cried. And of course, I cried. For the second time in my life, I experienced love at first sight. She was the prettiest, cutest, most amazing person I had ever seen. Her nostrils were shaped like little hearts. I couldn't stop staring at her.

Stephanie smiled at us with only one question on her mind, "How soon can my mom and I leave?"

"We're going to need to keep the baby overnight," the nurse said.

I stepped in. "We're the adoptive parents, so how does that work?"

Stephanie and Kamilla left while Sam and I stayed with Jaiden until the next morning, when we took our little girl home. We were a family. Looking back, I wonder if we wanted a baby to hold our relationship together. It's a tired old cliche, but it happens often enough, and I think that was probably part of our motivation. But I think a bigger part was love. From the time we met, we both knew we wanted a family. When you bring a child into the world, whether it's biologically yours or not, you're responsible for this little person. It certainly created a stronger bond between Sam and me. We instantly became a team, both of us wanting what was best for our little girl.

While Jaiden strengthened our relationship, having a newborn also created more challenges. It hit me hard that I was now a father, and I had another person to take care of and provide for. I had to be more successful and build a better life for her, not just better than the one I'd had when I was growing up - I wanted to give Jaiden the best life. I wanted to give her everything - the moon, the stars, the sun, and more.

I was still self-employed and the work was good, but my ambition ramped up, and pretty soon, I realized I could no longer handle it all on my own.

I'd met Ryan Brannigan through recreational baseball in 2009, and we'd become good friends. He tended to move from job to job, and during one game, I said, "I need help. Do you want to be a garage door technician?" He was my first employee. I bought a second truck. Business was taking off even more than it already had been, and the best part was that it was fun. I was full of energy, watching the business grow, knowing I was doing the best job in town.

Bringing Ryan on board was the first step in creating a real business. I was no longer just a guy with a truck. Having even one more person meant I could create a vision for it and make it big.

Sam was on maternity leave when Debbie came to visit and lend a hand. We'd been tossing around ideas for a middle name for Jaiden, and one day, something popped into my mind while I was driving to a job. I called Sam. "I think this might sound kind of weird and hippie, but what about Love? What about Jaiden Love Searles?"

"I love Love," Sam said, and that was her name.

When I got home that evening, Debbie asked, "How did you come up with that?"

"I love her so much already," I said. "And she's going to be surrounded by so much love as she grows up, it just fits." Today, thirteen years later, I call her Jaiden Love every day. I have memories from those early days that still make my heart swell, like lying with her in our bed, her body fitting perfectly from the palm of my hand to the crook of my elbow.

Jaiden helped heal our grief, perhaps even more for Sam than for me. She was born on April 25, and on November 5, 2012, we celebrated her "gotcha" day, the day the adoption became official.

Now that there was no chance of us losing her, we wanted to introduce her to everyone. We drove to Casper, Wyoming, to show her off to my parents, but they didn't even let us enter their house. Why couldn't we have adopted a baby who looked like us?

We'd never even thought about it. All Sam and I had wanted was a healthy baby. She could have been purple with yellow polka dots, and we would have been equally thrilled. I turned away from my parents' door, disappointed, but I wish I'd been more surprised than I was.

We then did the rounds of my friends and my grandparents. Everyone fell in love with her. Meeting her changed their lives. Growing up in Casper, they'd rarely seen an African American. They were rednecks living in a white town with all the prejudice that comes with that. My buddies - and me as well when I was young - used to use the "N" word carelessly and ignorantly. Moving to Colorado had changed that for me, but my buddies were still in Casper. But they didn't have to say anything to me when they met Jaiden. All I had to do was look at the light in their eyes to know they would never use that word again. That beautiful little black girl changed the community.

We celebrated Jaiden's first Christmas that year, and everything was right in our world. We were visiting with our friends again, fitting right in with the other young families.

In the spring of 2013, we went to Casper again because I was determined that my parents should meet Jaiden. I took her over to the house while Sam stayed behind at our friend's place. The front door was open. I saw my dad sitting on his old ratty chair through the screen door. "Can I come in?" I called to him.

"Yeah."

I walked in, letting the door flop closed behind me. I took a few steps toward him and placed Jaiden in his lap. His arms closed around her as I sat down on the hearth. My dad's face crumpled, tears leaking out of the corners of his eyes.

I saw racism leave his body. I watched his eyes change, his posture change, and his soul transform. I was witness to a blossoming of love. And we sat there in silence in that room that suddenly felt like a sacred space.

I had no idea then that he would soon leave this world. I'm so glad I was able to give him this gift before he died.

Perspective Shift

This chapter is where pain and purpose collided. After years of heartbreak, anger, and feeling like we were falling behind in the race of life, something bigger stepped in—love did. Love showed up not in the way we expected, but in the way we needed.

Sam and I had reached a breaking point. The pressure of infertility was crushing, the fights were raw, and Hawaii felt like the edge of the cliff. I'd never felt so hopeless and so desperate to make something work. Looking back, I can see how we weren't just grieving the inability to conceive—we were grieving the life we thought we were supposed to have.

The life we're meant for doesn't always look like the one we pictured. Sometimes it's even better.

Meeting Jaiden changed everything. From the moment we heard her cry, I knew I was holding a second chance, not just at fatherhood, but at life, healing, and family. And with that chance came a calling I hadn't fully understood until that moment:

To become the kind of father I always needed.

To break the cycle.

To love without conditions.

Jaiden was never just "our adopted daughter." She was our daughter, period. She didn't just fill a gap—she lit up the whole room. The world shifted the moment she entered it. Even my dad—whose entire life was shaped by his own pain and prejudice—softened in a single moment, holding her in his arms. I watched hate leave his body and love take its place.

That's the power of a child. That's the power of Jaiden Love.

And yeah, maybe we were hoping that a baby would save our marriage. But more than that, Jaiden reminded us of why we chose each other in the first place. She helped us remember that we're a team—one that's been through hell and keeps showing up anyway.

This chapter is a love letter. To Sam. To Jaiden. To healing. To the unexpected beauty that comes from broken places.

And to anyone wondering if their story is "off track"—let me say this:

Sometimes your "Plan B" is actually the miracle you didn't know you were praying for.

Garth Brooks said it best: "Some of God's greatest gifts are unanswered prayers."

Let's keep going.

—Trapper

CHAPTER 12

More Changes

In late 2013, I had a strong impulse to visit my dad. So we made the trip up to Casper, Wyoming. Once again, when I walked through the door, my dad was sitting in his old wagon-wheel leather chair, while I took a seat beside him on the fireplace hearth. We talked, probably about fairly inconsequential things, but my attention focused on his body, his face, and his aura that seemed to be fading in front of my eyes. He was wearing a moth-eaten gray shirt, old, ratty blue jeans, and work boots so ancient the toes were busted out of them. The stoop of his shoulders told me he was an old, run-down, hard-working man.

My mom was in another room, which probably gave my father the freedom to express what was weighing heavily on his mind. Leaning closer to me, and in a faint voice, he said, "I hope the day never comes when you realize you will never accomplish your dreams."

Hearing those words gave me chills; I understood he had given up on life. What had his dreams been? Whatever they were, they were out of reach. He had nothing to live for.

When I got the news in late March, a couple of months later, I was not surprised.

I was at a neighborhood party when my mom called at around midnight. I instantly heard the panic in her voice. "Your dad's in the hospital. You've got to come right away."

I found Sam in a crowd of women. "Sam, we've got to go right away."

Within an hour, we were on the road, tearing through the night and arriving at the hospital in Casper less than three hours later. Dad had suffered a massive heart attack and had already passed. He was only fifty-nine. Steve had also been fifty-nine. And suddenly - there it was - my own mortality staring down at me. I knew I'd better achieve as much as I possibly could before I was sixty. No waiting. No excuses. Do it now.

My father's death hit my mother hard, not just because she'd loved him so much, but because they'd been through so much together. They didn't have a lot of money, and how would she get through life without him? Her immediate question was, "Trapper, can you help me with...?" She needed a lot of help. I was happy to do what I could.

My father's death didn't have the emotional impact Steve's had. I'd been prepared for it. However, I again focused on taking care of whatever needed to be done. We had the funeral within two weeks. His friends said goodbye to him, and Sam and I went back home to live our lives.

I was strongly focused on my business. By this time, I had six employees and was still expanding. Our social life was also changing. Most of our friends were originally Sam's from college, and we'd usually see them for dinners or barbecues at one of our houses. At one point, someone said, "Wouldn't it be great if we lived close to each other?"

Nate and Leanne, our best "couple friends," bought a lot in Collier's Hill, a neighborhood in Erie, a suburban town twenty-seven miles north of Denver. They told us it was a great place to raise a family. Our house was close to a busy street, probably not the best place to raise a child. We were also in an excellent seller's market, so it made sense to sell, buy a lot, and build a house. So, we bought a lot just two over from Nate and Leanne, while another couple bought one only two blocks away, and we all started building our homes.

We were excited - a new start and a home designed exactly the way we wanted it. Everything else was falling into place, too. Sam loved her work, The Garage Doctor was scaling up, and I was doing well. Above all, we had Jaiden, the most wonderful child in the world.

In 2015, we moved into our beautiful new house. The only concern in my world was that our dogs, Gunner and Sophie, were getting older and having trouble navigating the stairs of our walk-out basement to access the backyard. It mattered because Gunner had been so important to me.

And then, in May 2015, my best friend Seth's father died. Around 2005, Seth's dad, JD, had been diagnosed with AML leukemia and was given a limited time to live. He underwent a successful bone marrow transplant but did suffer long-term complications with Graft vs Host. He passed away from complications related to colon cancer.

When we thought he was going to die after his leukemia diagnosis, we all came to the hospital: Seth, Seth's mother, Marianne, his sister Rachel, and his older half-brother, Tanner. After talking to us, JD asked to speak to each of us individually. When it was my turn to be alone with him, he told me he was proud of me. Not even my own father had never said those words to me.

JD was the first person in my life who had served as a mentor and a father figure. He taught me how to be in the world and even introduced me to personal hygiene.

When he died, it felt like a huge chunk of my life had broken off. First Steve, then my father, and then JD. Each left a void. I had no one to fill this third big one.

Seth was hugely impacted, although he wasn't the kind of guy to show it. But I knew that inside, Seth was hurting. We both were. And we questioned, how could JD have overcome leukemia, and then get this second diagnosis? It wasn't fair!

Seth and I leaned on each other during that time, and I think it helped us face the world without JD. But we missed him dearly, especially Seth. I know his father's death hit him hard. It's true, but sad that so often we don't know what we have until it's gone.

I'd already lost Steve, and JD's passing hit me hard. These two men had been my biggest role models. I'd looked up to them and loved them, and now they were gone. Had I appreciated them enough while they were alive? How was I supposed to navigate the future without them?

But through all that grief, Sam and I settled into our new home, thinking how lucky we were to live there. We realized pretty quickly that our neighborhood was not what we'd thought it would be. Our neighbors were almost uniformly status-seekers. Everyone was acutely aware of what everyone else had or did and felt a desperate need to keep up.

I didn't care. If I wanted something, I would simply go out and buy it. It didn't concern me who had a new Porsche or a John Deere riding lawn mower. I was just a hard-working, ambitious blue-collar guy. If we got together with new friends in the neighborhood, I did my best to steer clear of conversations involving what the latest new toy someone had acquired was, or how exciting it was that they were going to Bali for Christmas, and what were our plans? I had no aspirations to slide into that level of pretentiousness.

Our neighbors would buy their "toys" to impress others. Sam and I spent money because, by now, we had a good chunk of it, but we weren't doing it for others. When I bought nice things, it was to prove to myself that I could do it. I didn't have to show it off for the neighbors to see.

My greatest ambition was to keep my family afloat. When we'd bought our lot and started building, I'd also purchased a commercial building for my business. Until then, I'd been running it out of my home. That was no longer feasible. I couldn't run The Garage Doctor from a distance. Every day was busy, especially because I still had no idea how to run a business. I was winging it every day, hiring people who happened to be available, rather than thoroughly vetting them. Whenever I hired someone, I had to buy another truck, and my debts started piling up. And now we had a bigger mortgage, and the financial stress was digging into me.

In 2015, Sam started talking to me about making some changes." You need to be around more," she said. "You're working too much. Jaiden needs you to be there more often."

She had a point. One Saturday, I woke up at about 5.30 a.m. to get ready for work. Jaiden, who was tucked in with us, rolled over to Sam and said, "Mommy, why do you and I get weekends and Daddy doesn't?"

Her words echoed in my head all day.

When I got home that night, Sam said, "Hey, we've got to figure some stuff out. You're working too much."

I agreed. "I know. I'm just grinding away, trying to get us to a great future."

It didn't even occur to me that Sam and I hadn't ever talked about our goals. What did we want? What were we striving for? We had a vague notion that we were working hard to create a better lifestyle, but what was the bigger context?

In October of that year, we visited Seth and Stacey in Casper. We checked into a Holiday Inn and drove to their place for a big Halloween bash. Jaiden ran off to play with the other kids, and Sam and I headed for the bar. I poured myself a soda water, the only one there who wasn't drinking. When Sam drank, she was a lot of fun, more social and flirty, except on this occasion. She just seemed uncharacteristically distant. I didn't think much of it as I walked around the house, talking to all my good friends.

At one point, I wandered downstairs. Sam was sitting on the couch, smiling at her phone, thumbs moving.

"Who are you texting?" I asked. "Everyone we know is here."

"I'm just texting Taylor," she said.

Taylor? Why would she be texting her brother?

I leaned forward to have a look at her screen. She moved the phone away, shielding it with her arm.

She was pretty drunk by now, and I thought something odd was going on. "Babe, who are you texting? Give me your phone."

I reached for it, and she pulled it away from me, holding it close to her. What the fuck? We'd never had online secrets. We'd never cared about phone privacy. I grabbed the phone out of her hands.

"I had such a great conversation with you the other night."

"You brought back all those butterflies in my stomach that I used to feel for you."

There were more, including texts that ended with "I love you."

I stood frozen in place, surrounded by all my friends, looking at my wife who was seeing another man.

I had only one thought: *You just ruined my life.*

I read a few more texts, turned to Sam, tossed the phone back at her, and said, "I'm leaving right now." I walked upstairs and into an empty bedroom to catch my breath. I didn't have time to sort through a chaos of emotions: I was devastated, sad, angry, betrayed, and physically sick. We'd invested years in each other. Had it all been a waste? Why?

Sam rushed in after me. "You're overreacting."

"How am I overreacting? I just read a message from you to your boyfriend. This is horse shit! Why are you even talking with this guy?"

She had nothing to say.

"I'm going back to the hotel, I'm going to pack, and I'm going home with Jaiden," I said.

Sam started yelling. I don't remember her words, only the almost hysterical, angry feelings behind them.

Seth must have heard, because he came stumbling in, totally hammered.

"Get the fuck out of here," I said. "You don't know what's going on here, but this is real life shit that's going down. Sam and I are not going to be okay after this. I just caught her cheating!"

"She would never do that!" Seth said, slurring his words. "She's the best thing that's ever happened to you in your whole life. You're out of line!" Seth and I then got into a little pushing match, he being stronger than me, threw me into a dresser. I must have gone unconscious for a minute or two, and when I came to, I was bleeding around my left eye.

What? I was out of line? I was the only sober adult in the house, and I'd just found out my wife was having an affair!

"You need to get out of here," I told him.

The bedroom door opened again, and our friend, PJ, walked in. PJ was a huge guy, about six feet four inches and built like a mixed martial arts fighter.

"What's going on?" He was slurring his words, too.

"Sam's cheating on me!"

"Trapper - she would never do that to you."

"Listen, fuckers, this is real life - and my life just got destroyed - just now. So get out of my life. I don't need to deal with this shit!"

I looked around the room. Everyone was standing. No one was getting out. Okay, fine, I spun around on my heels, grabbed the doorknob, yanked the door open, and walked right out of the room, down the hall, and out of the house. PJ was right behind me, grabbed hold of my arm, and stopped me cold.

"Dude," I said. "Let me leave!"

The lights went on in the house across the street. An older man came out on the porch, still wrapping a bathrobe around himself. He took one look at the scene and called out, "You guys need to keep it down!"

I turned around as much as I could, given PJ's iron grip. "PJ! Get off me!"

PJ picked me up at least as high as his chest, my arms and legs flailing. He gave one mighty heave and threw me to the ground. Instant pain and a certain knowledge - *something's wrong with me.* I gasped for air through the pressure in my chest. PJ threw himself on top of me.

"PJ," I gasped. "I can't breathe. Get off me. You're going to kill me!"

The neighbor yelled from across the street, "I'm calling the cops!"

PJ pushed himself to his feet, looked down at me, grunted, and turned and walked back into the house.

I staggered to my feet. Something was wrong. The pressure inside my chest was building. And then a wave of nausea washed over me. I lifted a hand to my face to wipe away the sweat. It came away streaked with blood. Not knowing what to do, I stumbled down the street in the direction of my buddy Jared's house. The pain from my chest was now radiating into the rest of my body.

I felt a small tug on my arm. I turned my head. Jolene, PJ's wife, had caught up with me. "Trapper, come back to the house. The cops are coming. This is bad."

"I don't give a fuck," I said. "I didn't do anything wrong, and I'm not going back in that fucking house."

Lights flashing, the first police car pulled up, then a second, and then a fire truck and an ambulance. One police car pulled up to the house. The other stopped beside me, and I recognized a guy I'd played baseball with in high school.

"Trapper," he said. "You're in rough shape. You look like you were in a fight."

"Not a fight," I said. "PJ threw me down."

"Oh my god! PJ did this?"

"Yeah."

"Well, just so you know, he's on thin ice with the law. He's been getting into fights. Do you want to press charges?"

I was not about to turn in a friend. "No, it's not a big deal," I said. "They're drunk and being stupid, but they're my friends. My wife and I are having an issue right now, and I'm just trying to make it to my hotel."

Then the other cop walked over from the house, saying he'd heard there was a domestic dispute. Then the EMTs checked me out, insisting they wanted to take me to the hospital. The first policeman said, "If they hospitalize you, we have to write up a report naming who did this."

"Then I'm not going to the hospital," I said.

"Trapper," the EMT said. "We think you have multiple broken ribs. Your lungs are not in good shape."

"I'm going back to my hotel," I said.

The cop drove me to my hotel. An hour later, Sam and Jaiden arrived. I was in the shower, watching blood from the gash in my head swirling down the drain. I'd felt desperate, sad, awful and downright shitty in my life, but this was the worst I'd ever been.

I came out of the shower. "We need to talk when we get home," I told Sam. "But I'm going to bed now."

The next morning, we drove home in uneasy silence. My doctor told me I had five broken ribs, making breathing painful for two months. But the physical pain was nothing compared to the emotional agony. The only way I knew to handle that was to become an investigative reporter. I had to know what was going on between Sam and the guy she said "I love you" to, and I was ready to do anything to know the truth.

Perspective Shift

This chapter was a storm.

It started with quiet—my dad's tired voice, worn down by dreams he'd surrendered—and ended in chaos: betrayal, grief, broken ribs. But now I see it wasn't about destruction. It was about clarity—the kind only loss can bring.

When my dad said, "I hope there's never a day you realize that your dreams are out of reach," I felt the weight of his surrender... and my warning.

So I did what I knew: I built. I grew. I worked harder.

But while my outer world expanded, my inner world unraveled—my marriage, my community, my peace. I lost Steve, then my dad, and then JD, the first man who showed me how to stand tall. There were no more mentors, and no one left to look up to. I had to become that man now... but I didn't know how.

So I kept grinding. And it cost me.

Jaiden's voice—"Why do you and I get weekends and Daddy doesn't?"—cut deep. But still, I didn't slow down. I didn't know how.

Then came Halloween.

That night didn't just break my heart. It broke the illusion I'd clung to—that hard work, loyalty, and love would keep me safe. It didn't. I was sober, surrounded by friends, and I still left bleeding.

That night gave me clarity. It showed me what I'd tolerated—and who I was becoming. Not a victim. Not a broken man. But a father, a husband, a leader who would never again let someone else define his worth.

This chapter was hell.

Let's keep going.

—Trapper

CHAPTER 13

Unravelling

I started relentlessly questioning Sam. "How long have you been doing this? Who is this man? Why are you doing this?"

I had no more trust - not a shred. I didn't believe a word she said. Every time she picked up her phone, I asked. "Who are you calling? Are you texting him?"

My overriding thought was that I had to fix whatever had gone wrong in my marriage. If it was broken, clearly I was accountable for that, and I had to repair the damage I had caused. I hired *Tap the Potential,* a company offering business coaching that would help me design a sustainably profitable business that would also allow me to better manage and balance my time. Sam gave me a list of the things she asked me to change. She wanted more help around the house and more involvement with Jaiden. It all made sense to me. It was true that I'd been pouring most of my energy into work. I needed to give more of myself to my family. I was still angry, but I was convinced it would dissipate if I could get our marriage back on track.

In addition to the coaching, I started seeing my therapist again, hoping I could become a better man. If I could improve, then Sam wouldn't have to look outside her marriage for what she needed. I had my moments of self-pity, too, where I would ask, "What did I do to deserve this? I didn't think I was such a terrible husband."

I knew I wasn't the best, but I was a good provider and a good dad. I was a good everything - I just wasn't a great everything. I was the handyman of husbands.

I dove headfirst into "self-improvement." I changed my work routine to free up more time to be present with my family. I tried to do everything Sam wanted me to, determined to be what and who she wanted me to be.

I had only one request for Sam: never talk to this guy again.

At about that time, we moved again, selling our house at Collier's Hill to move back to Westminster to a big house on an acre of land. Our neighborhood in Erie had never been right for us, and once I discovered that it appeared to be the divorce capital of the state, I wanted out.

In 2017, we took a trip to Amish country in Missouri to visit my Uncle Robert for Thanksgiving. I hooked up a fifth wheel to our truck, and we hit the road. We resolved to create a great family memory. We drove through Kansas City, arriving at Uncle Robert's hundred-acre spread where we set up our camper for a few days. Uncle Robert was a Navy veteran with a big collection of firearms and a beautiful, spacious log house. He, my cousins, and I bonded over target shooting.

That Thursday, we had a big Thanksgiving dinner at about 3 p.m., and then my stomach pains started. They were bad enough that I went back to the camper to rest. I dozed off and didn't wake up until the next morning.

Feeling reasonably fine, I got behind the wheel and we started our return drive. Back home, Sam got in the shower, and her phone rang. I answered, "This is Sam's phone."

The caller hung up.

I recognized a Washington State area code.

Sam came out of the bathroom.

"Sam, call this number back for me, okay?"

She hit the dial button. The man answered. A red-hot anger took complete possession of my body. Every limb was shaking. I had just enough presence of mind to call my sister and ask her to come and pick Jaiden up. "Sam and I are going to have a rough night."

Amber was there in about forty-five minutes. I gave her a brief explanation of the situation. "You should leave her," she said.

How could I leave Sam when I was so in love with her? But I was also in a rage. I don't recall the words I said that night. I know they were as hurtful as I could make them. I know I threw a television through a second-floor window. I know I exhausted every four-letter word in my vocabulary at least two or three times over.

Finally, I called Sam's mother, Debbie. "She did it again," I said. "What the fuck! This is ridiculous!"

I grilled Sam, and she admitted that she had been talking to the man since 2012, five years after we got married. "Why didn't you talk to this guy before then? What made you send him a picture of yourself wearing lingerie in 2012? Who is this guy?"

The more I found out, the angrier I got. Sam confessed the man had been her childhood sweetheart. And why hadn't she been in touch with him before 2012? Because he'd been in jail for grand larceny auto and assaulting a police officer. He was an ex-con, and she preferred him to me? Maybe I wouldn't have been quite as angry or devastated if he'd been a doctor or a lawyer - at least pick someone better than me. But an ex-con? Was this the only reason she was with me and not him, because he'd been unavailable?

I was ruined, but I had enough awareness left inside to say to Sam, "You need help. You need to figure out your shit. I'm an awesome dude. I've done everything to be the man you want. I've worked so hard so we could live in this gorgeous neighborhood. I'm busting my ass to create opportunities for us, and you're being selfish. You need to figure out your shit, or I'm going to leave."

Debbie arrived, sharing her insights about relationships and explaining how they could sometimes be challenging.

"But this isn't just hard," I said. "This is really shitty. What your daughter is doing to me is destroying my life."

We tried. Sam went to therapy, I continued with my therapist, and we went to couples therapy together. My request was just as simple as before. "You've just got to stop talking to this guy. That's all I need you to do. Don't speak to him. He's a homewrecker."

Sam protested: he'd never been her boyfriend. They'd known each other since childhood and had always had a strong connection. He would simply pop in and out of her life. My take on that? He popped in and out because he didn't mind breaking up a family. "He doesn't care about you," I told her. "You're just a tool. When he's not getting what he needs from the local baristas at Starbucks, he turns to you."

I could have left. So many people thought I should have. But I loved Sam so much. I think some of my friends lost respect for me because I wasn't showing enough respect for myself. But I had to do what I felt was right, and that was loving Sam. I respected myself, but I loved Sam more.

I didn't connect the dots at the time to the troubles in my relationship with Sam and the constant battles my parents fought. That's so much easier to do in hindsight: my unquestioning love for Sam, just like my parents' for each other, and the trust issues. My mother never trusted my dad, following him everywhere, including on his jobs. I had no trust in Sam. None. I wanted to be Sam's priority. I wasn't. It hurt like a knife in my heart.

We worked on our marriage, including doing couples therapy. Sam also sought counseling on her own, feeling that she needed to address some of her own issues. Our work still consumed a lot of our time, and often I was just too tired to work on the relationship. I'd come home and just want to sleep.

And the man lived in Washington state, not next door. We could survive this, but I had to create some rules like, "You can't travel to Washington, and you can't be on social media. No Facebook or Twitter or Instagram, because he will find you, and you will make a bad decision because you don't have any self-control, and you don't have enough respect for our relationship."

That sounds intensely controlling, but I didn't know any other way to make my soul feel safe. I couldn't trust Sam. I was trying to make myself feel secure. I hated it. We'd always felt so free with each other and about each other. I had never wanted to be in a marriage like my parents, where I was so insecure that I had to make rules. But here I was.

We were out with friends one evening when they discovered I didn't allow Sam on social media. "Why are you so controlling with Sam?"

"You want to know why I feel I have to control Sam's shit?" I asked. "Because she makes bad fucking decisions and she cheated on me."

After the initial shock of my outburst, they said, "Oh no, there's no way Sam would do that; she's the sweetest person."

"Yes, she is," I said. "But she's also an adulterer and a habitual liar. That's my wife. You can judge me if you want, but I'm the one who lives with her."

A funny thing happened after my outburst. Friends started taking sides, but a certain vulnerability showed up among the men who felt that if I could open up like that, so could they. One of them said to me, "I think my wife is cheating too."

It also brought a new awareness to the group that we often judge without truly knowing all the facts about the situation.

I started withdrawing from our group, wondering if they really were friends. I noticed that because Sam and I had a swimming pool, they all wanted one too. And because I was driving an Aston Martin, they wanted a hot sports car. Were they so discontent with their own lives that they just needed more status to make it all okay? Yes, I bought material things because I wanted to bury the feelings that came with all of life's traumas. But at least I knew that's what I was doing. I didn't know how to do it differently. I didn't know how to ease the pain, and I certainly had no clue how to love myself.

In our own messy way, we continued to go to our jobs and carry on with our lives. And then, in early 2021, Sam and I flew to Scottsdale, Arizona, one of our favorite places, where we reconnected and had a beautiful, romantic time.

The night we got back, Sam got into the shower. I was in the bedroom when I saw Sam's phone flashing. What was that? An icon! I tapped it to reveal a kaleidoscope of photos and videos of her that Sam had been sending to the man in Washington.

I was beyond angry. I texted her mom, Debbie, forwarded the photos to her, and said, "I think I'm going to leave Sam. I don't deserve this. I deserve the best wife. I've done so many things right, and I've accomplished so much for us, and this happens? Is all I'm doing not good enough? All the effort I'm putting into being a great husband isn't good enough?"

Sam came out of the bathroom, wrapped in her terry robe. She looked at me. "What's wrong?"

"I think you need to talk to your mom."

Debbie had helped keep us together so often, reminding us that marriage requires work. She had faith in us. Could she work her magic again? But now I was full of doubts. Had Debbie persuaded Sam to stay in the marriage while Sam only wanted to get out?

I'd said to Debbie once, "If Sam doesn't want to be married to me anymore, just tell me. That's fine. We'll end it."

Debbie always said that Sam loved me and wanted to be with me. I had evidence to the contrary, but I couldn't let her go – not the first time the issue had raised its head, and not now.

A few days later, Sam was let go, one of several people her company had to let go due to COVID-19 restrictions. She sank into depression, but I suspect I was the only one who recognized the signs. Sam was so good at hiding those feelings. When Debbie arrived a few days later, she told Sam, "If Trapper chooses to stay, and you do this one more time, and he leaves, I'm writing you out of my will."

I couldn't carry out the threat I'd voiced to Debbie. I still loved Sam beyond reason. She started seeing her therapist again, who put her on antidepressants. It made a difference, but it certainly didn't fix our issues. We were living as roommates, and I was more and more unhappy, particularly with myself.

I needed to get away. The fishing trip I had planned with my buddies couldn't have come at a better time. It turned out to be far more than a small outdoor adventure with good friends.

Perspective Shift

This chapter is about clinging to hope when everything in you knows it's time to let go. It's about fighting with everything you've got to save something that's already bleeding out.

Back then, I thought if I just worked harder on the business, on myself, on the relationship, I could fix it. I believed that if I could show up better, love more fully, and become the man Sam wanted, then maybe she'd see me again the way I saw her. But what I've come to realize is... You can't outwork someone else's unhealed pain.

I wasn't just heartbroken—I was shattered. And when I finally said, "You've got to stop talking to this guy," I wasn't trying to control Sam. I was just a man trying to protect what little was left of his dignity. But the truth? I didn't feel safe. And I didn't know how to rebuild trust without her fully and consistently choosing our marriage.

I lost friends because of that choice. Some questioned my manhood. Others called me blind. But no one else lived in my skin. No one else saw the woman I fell in love with. I was fighting for that version of Sam, even though she'd become someone I no longer recognized.

And in fighting for her, I lost track of myself.

That's the part that stings most. Because when I look back now, I can see how hard I tried to be the man everyone needed me to be. The good husband. The great dad. The successful entrepreneur. But I never stopped to ask— what about me? What do I need? What do I deserve?

I deserve honesty. I deserve loyalty. I deserve love.

It wasn't just my marriage that was unraveling. It was my sense of self.

This chapter is messy. There's no ribbon to tie it up neatly. Just a raw, bleeding truth that I was hanging onto something that no longer felt like love, but obligation. I stayed when most would have run. And maybe that makes me foolish. But maybe it also makes me real.

That's why that fishing trip mattered.

Because out there, in nature, with people who didn't expect me to be anything but myself... I started to remember who I was before all the damage. And I started to wonder who I could become if I finally stopped trying to fix what was already broken.

Let's keep going.

—**Trapper**

CHAPTER 14

Life and Death

A few days before leaving on my fishing trip, I noticed Sam's diary on her bedside table. I couldn't resist picking it up. Maybe it would give me some clues about what I could do to make our lives better. I was only going to read an entry or two, but once that Pandora's box was open, I couldn't put the lid back on.

What I read hurt more than all the text messages I'd found on her phone. These were her thoughts, raw and honest. I read pages of, "I wish I was brave enough to leave Trapper and take Jaiden to Seattle. I wish it were just Jaiden and me. If it were just me and Jaiden, we could move to Seattle to be with him."

Page after page ripped my heart out. How could she continue like this if she was so unhappy? I believed if I was that dissatisfied with my life, I'd stop and change it. By the time I closed the journal and put it back, my sadness was resting on my chest like a stone. I got up, walked into my office, and checked my life insurance policies. I'd have to make my death look like an accident.

That man in Seattle - he'd ruined my life. I had nothing left to live for. It was easier to put the onus on the man and not Sam. It took time for me to look back and realize that Sam was making decisions about how she wanted to be in our relationship. All her actions were her choice. But sitting in my den that day, all I could think was that I wanted a bus to run over him.

I knew that Sam had to hate me to write what she did. She would be so much happier without me. I loved her more than myself - more than life. I could give her the gift of taking me out of the picture, and she would never have to know it was a deliberate act. She'd be free to live the life she wanted.

It was a beautiful September day when we set out on our fishing trip. The sky was the purest blue, broken by a few small, lazy clouds drifting on a warm breeze. Tall cottonwoods and pines lined the mountain road that snaked up over the pass and down into the canyon, where the Colorado River meandered between red rock walls.

We set up camp on a pebble beach, pulled out the rafts, and launched onto the water. We dropped our lines, not really caring if we caught anything, the warm sun beating down making us as lazy as the low-buzzing blue bottle flies. After drifting downstream, we pulled up on a beach near tall cliffs where we would watch the cliff jumpers who were daring enough to toss themselves off the edge to plunge into the pools far below.

I'd always been afraid of heights. Cliff jumping was something I had never considered, but today, I knew it didn't matter if I lived or died. "I'm going to jump," I told my buddies.

"What?"

"I'm going to do that."

I climbed to my feet and scaled the almost vertical rock to the top of the cliff. I should have been afraid. My legs should have been wobbly with nerves, and any other time they would have been. Not today. Today was my last day. I looked up at the sky and down at the water, so far down. A deep sense of peace was all I felt. I walked to the edge - no pause or hesitation. I closed my eyes and jumped.

Weightless. Free. Peaceful.

Boom!

I was in the water, going down and down. For how long? It felt like forever. I kicked and pulled with my arms, surfaced, and took a huge gulp of air. I heard my friends hollering and cheering. The sense of peace burrowed deeper inside me.

We got back in our rafts and pointed ourselves to our camping spot, where we cooked a great steak dinner and cracked a few beers, watching the stars blink themselves into a velvet sky. While my friends continued to chat around the campfire, I told them I was heading back up the mountain in the truck, where

I'd have a cell signal to call home. They knew I always checked in, so they waved me off.

I drove back up the mountain, my mind empty, my heart at peace. I felt no regrets about leaving this beautiful earth. I had no sorrow about my life. I'd already shed all the tears I needed to in the last three years. I was certain about what came next. I had only one more loose end to tie up - a call to Jaiden to tell her I loved her - and to hear her voice one more time.

I drove up the switchbacks we'd come down earlier that day, my headlights picking up the silvery shadows of the cottonwoods, and the skittering of little nighttime critters, disappearing over the edge of the dropoff. On the drive in, I'd chosen my spot. At the top of the mountain was a mile-long straightaway where I could pick up speed. At the end of the mile was a sharp curve with a low guardrail that didn't stand a chance of holding up against my 2019 F450 Dually with a four-inch lift.

The fact it was night stood in my favor. I couldn't see past my headlights. The darkness was absolute. When the truck went over, I would have no reason to be afraid. All I would see was blackness. I would literally sail out into the void.

No fear. No anticipation of an impact. When the impact came, it would come, and I would be gone.

I arrived at the flat top of the mountain, where I picked up a cell signal and called Jaiden. I wanted our last conversation to be normal and loving. I asked about her day, and she asked about mine. I told her about the beauty of the river and my daring cliff jump. After about fifteen minutes, I said, "I love you. See you on Monday."

"I love you, too. Do you want to talk to Mom?"

"No. I'm good. Just gonna go."

I hung up. That was enough. That was all I'd needed. She and Sam would be all right. And then I didn't think about them at all. I didn't worry about their future or what they would do. I thought only about myself. It flashed through my mind that this was the first time in my life I'd been completely selfish. I'd always known how I felt. I'd always been able to put a name to my emotions, but I'd rarely acted on them, and never wholeheartedly. I'd been too busy caring for others to take care of myself.

That was about to change. For one time in my life, I was focused only on myself.

I put my foot on the gas, watching the shapes of the tall trees flying by— faster and faster. I watched the needle climb to a hundred forty, anticipating the turn and the guardrail. There it was. My deep peace reached profound new depths.

My navigation screen lit up: "Phone call from Stinkybean," my pet name for Jaiden.

I braked. The truck stopped about a car's length from the guardrail. Still very much at peace, I answered, "Hey, Stink. What's up? Are you okay?"

"Dad, you just didn't sound like yourself earlier. I want you to come home tonight."

I hung up. Okay. If Jaiden wanted me to come home, I was going home. She needed me. Nothing was more important than that.

I drove back to the camp, packed up, and drove back to Denver. Feelings that had been lurking under my blanket of peace started to surface. I wiped away tears. But what were these emotions? Was I sad? Regretful? I didn't know what to call them - I could only feel them. As I got closer to home, I understood that even if Sam hated me and didn't want to be with me, Jaiden loved me. I had friends who loved me. Maybe I could let Sam go and still have a lot to live for.

I called my therapist, Tamara, on my cell phone and told her what had happened.

"Are you still thinking about hurting yourself?" she asked.

"No."

"Are you thinking about hurting anybody else?"

"No."

I understood then that because Jaiden had called back, I would have the opportunity to live the rest of my life. I might have felt that my whole life was being destroyed, but it was only a small part that was lying in ruins.

It's hard to write about this because I'm alive today, and I know how the rest of my story plays out. I wish I could go back to that other me, hug him, and reassure him, "Your life is worth living—more than you can possibly know right now."

I pulled up in front of our house and walked through the front door. Jaiden was asleep. Sam was still up. I told her, "I read a lot of your diary. And so, I attempted to take my life earlier tonight."

If I'd had fantasies about her loving reactions, they died instantly. She listened and nodded. She didn't cry. She didn't say she was sorry. A familiar weight of sadness settled down in my chest.

The next day, we talked. The big question hanging between us was, "Where do we go from here?" We had no answers.

At about midnight, I called Nate, who had been on the fishing trip. "Can you come over? I need to talk."

He came: no questions asked. When I told him about my attempted suicide, I only had to look at his face to see his hurt. "You're like my brother," he said. "That would have been so painful for my family and my boys - and for your family."

His words helped me recognize I had some worth - maybe not to Sam, but to other people who cared about me. Talking to Tamara, my therapist, also helped. I could sense something significant shifting within me. For the first time, instead of asking myself what I could do to make Sam happy, I asked, "What can I do to take care of myself?"

I let Sam go. She would have to look after herself. I had to focus on myself. Step by step, I was walking down a new road where I was going to create the best version of me. I had done everything I could to create a great lifestyle and a loving family, and I'd failed because I hadn't put myself into the scenario. I was determined to change that.

Sam didn't want to talk about that night on the mountain, but we did, and it helped us both. With my therapist's guidance, I took more and more steps that focused on my well-being. I started working out and getting into better shape. If I felt frustrated, I went to the gym.

In late 2021, about three months after the fishing trip, Sam and I started talking more about our relationship. When we did, I remembered to focus not just on Sam, but also on what was important to me. What did I love about myself?

I used to worry about Sam almost obsessively."Sam, what can I do for you? What can I do to make you happy? What can I do to help you?"

I started asking what I could do for myself to make myself happy. Sam was not my problem anymore. She was her own person who needed to figure out what would make her happy. If she wanted me to be part of her life, that was great. If not, I was going to be just fine. I even considered that Sam and I would be better off apart. I was feeling good about who I was and what I was doing. I was proud of the successful business I had built, and all the love and care I had put into my family.

At the end of that year, we went to Disneyland in Florida, and that's when we started talking about our future for the first time. Did we have a future together?

It was a question we had to answer.

Perspective Shift

This chapter is a turning point—not just in the narrative, but in the story of my soul.

I didn't write it from a place of drama. I wrote it from peace. Because when I was up on that mountain road, staring at the curve and the guardrail, I wasn't panicking. I wasn't desperate. I was done. There was no more fight left in me. I truly believed the kindest, most generous thing I could do for Sam, Jaiden, and everyone was to quietly remove myself from the equation.

That's how distorted my perspective had become. That's how heavy the weight of heartbreak, betrayal, and unhealed pain had grown.

I wasn't choosing death because I hated life. I was choosing death because I loved them too much and couldn't see how I belonged anymore.

And then... Jaiden called.

In one breath, she brought me home—not just physically, but emotionally, spiritually, and mentally. She tethered me back to purpose and reminded me of the most profound truth I had forgotten. I mattered.

That call didn't just stop the truck. From that moment, something deep began to shift—not immediately, not perfectly, but permanently.

I'd spent so many years trying to be everything for everyone, especially Sam. But it wasn't until I faced death that I realized: I'd never really shown up for myself.

This chapter isn't about suicide. It's about awakening. It's about the moment you realize that taking care of your heart isn't selfish—it's sacred. That your worth doesn't disappear when someone stops seeing it. That even when love feels one-sided or loyalty goes unreciprocated, you still get to love yourself.

Jaiden's phone call saved my life—but I saved my own soul by deciding to live.

That shift—from "How do I keep Sam happy?" to "How do I keep myself whole?"—wasn't just survival. It was the start of something extraordinary. Something real. Something that is mine.

And that was the moment I finally began to rise.

Let's keep going.

—**Trapper**

CHAPTER 15

Emergency

Sam and I decided that if we were going to stay together, perhaps we should try dating again first. Sam was seeing a therapist and taking antidepressants. The combination was making a big difference to her moods, and she started feeling pretty good about herself. We began going out and discussing our future, something we had never done before. Even through our rough times, we had never sat down and wrestled with our issues. We'd just let life carry us forward. We were busy. There was never time to just talk.

We scheduled weekly dates just for the two of us, when all we did was talk about our hopes and dreams and the future we envisioned. We had never discussed our life goals. What did we want to achieve? What were our needs inside our marriage? What did we want out of our relationship? Where did we want to live? Even that was up for discussion because neither of us liked Colorado, but we did love Arizona.

We even talked about the guy in Seattle. We'd avoided so many subjects, and that was a big one. Why? That was my big question. Why did she need this person in her life? Sam couldn't answer. She was asking her therapist the same question. Why was this man important to her?

I still had an uneasy feeling in the pit of my stomach. I was still insecure, still struggling with trying to understand, but Sam couldn't reassure me. She had no answers either. But the more we talked, the better we felt about each other. Our love was still alive, and we decided our marriage was worth saving.

I never stopped loving her.

In February 2022, Sam, Jaiden, and I went to Scottsdale, which remains our favorite place to vacation. A month later, Sam and I flew down again on our own and started talking about buying a condo or an Airbnb as a permanent vacation home. Life felt the way I'd always thought it should. My business was doing well, too. But I also knew I didn't want to own the Garage Doctor much longer. It was eating up too much of my time, time I should be spending with my family. I recognized I needed to create a different framework for the company so it could essentially run itself. Ideally, I could be minimally involved while it still created a good revenue. I hired people who could run the business and do it well, and that led to good sustainability.

After our second trip to Arizona, we booked airline tickets for another trip to Arizona on April 25 to look at properties with a real estate agent. We were excited as we counted down the days.

On April 11, my best friend Seth and his wife visited. We had dinner at the Bao Brewhouse in downtown Denver and then went to a Broadway show. I remember thinking that this was the way life should be—and it could only get better. The next weekend, on April 16, Sam had tickets for *Jersey Boys*, my favorite Broadway show. Before the show, we went to dinner at Ocean Prime with our friends Ryan and Chelsea, and Brad and Julie.

Just as we sat down, I saw Sam lean over and grab the right side of her head.

"Are you all right?" I asked.

"I just need to go to the bathroom," she said.

Five or more minutes passed. Where was Sam? I texted. "Are you okay?"

No reply.

I got up, walked to the back of the restaurant, and knocked on the door of the ladies' room. No answer. I pushed it open. Sam was leaning against a stall door, beads of sweat on her forehead and running down her chin. A puddle of vomit was congealing on the tiled floor.

A knot of worry tightened my gut. "Sam, are you okay?"

She squinted at me. "Who are you?"

I panicked, ran back to our table, and said, "Brad, I need your keys. I think Sam's dying."

"What!"

We dashed back to the ladies room. She was slumped against the wall, drifting in and out of consciousness. We got her out of the restaurant. While the valet was retrieving the car, Sam vomited again and again. She didn't recognize us or even herself.

"Brad," I said. "I've got to go."

"Go," he said. "Take the car."

The only hospital I knew about was near our house, a thirty-minute drive. I got there in eleven minutes, flew into the emergency room, and yelled, "I think my wife's dying! I need help! Right now!"

Someone grabbed a wheelchair and got her inside. The desk clerks insisted on registering her. I wasn't going to put up with that BS. "She needs help right now!" I said. "She's coming in and out of consciousness. She doesn't know who she is. She can't talk!"

I desperately wanted to be calm and coherent, but I knew we were running out of time.

"Calm down, sir," the receptionist said.

Not a chance. I spotted a doctor walking by. "Hey! I said, jumping in front of him. "These guys are fucking with me and my wife is dying."

"Who's your wife?"

I led him to her.

His assessment was instant. "She needs an MRI and a CT scan right now!" he said. "Right now!"

They wheeled her around the corner to the CT scan. Seven or eight minutes later, the doctor came out. "We have to life-flight her to Central. She's not in good shape. She needs emergency surgery."

But what was wrong with her?

No one knew, but they were certain it was life-threatening.

I called Nate to drive me to St. Anthony Central Hospital. While waiting for him to arrive, I got Sam checked in. Minutes later, the doctor approached me. "You might want to walk out with us to the helicopter. We don't know if she's going to make it."

I walked beside the gurney, memorizing every line and plane of her face. I bent down, kissed her, and said, "I love you." She opened her eyes and smiled - the last time I ever saw that particular smile. I watched the helicopter lift into the sky. Would I see her alive again?

My friends drove me to the hospital. She was already in surgery when I got there forty minutes later. A neurologist told me the initial findings were serious. "It's a long road," he said. "But first, we just have to get through tonight. It's going to be one day at a time."

I sat in the waiting room, thinking of all the time we had wasted - all the fighting, arguing, and escaping each other, when we could have been loving each other. What was life? It was the most fragile of gifts that could shatter in an instant.

I couldn't imagine life without Sam in it. At that moment, nothing mattered except her.

For thirteen days, I never left the hospital. Seth drove from Casper to Denver to be with me. I don't know how many days and nights he was by my side, but wherever I looked up, there he was. Then Sam's mother, Debbie, arrived to help keep the vigil.

I slept in the waiting room through surgeries and procedures that never seemed to end. Her initial injury was a subarachnoid hemorrhage, a bleeding in the space between the brain and the membrane that covers it. On April 17, the day after her initial surgery, the doctors explained that Sam's aneurysm was rare and of an odd shape that required inserting a stent to eliminate the bleeding. She went into surgery that day for a craniectomy to remove the top quarter portion of her skull to ease the swelling in her brain. The pressure inside her skull could easily have killed her.

They told us they had to get the bleeding down, and she would be in critical condition for some time. The next day, on the eighteenth, they discovered another bleed, but they could only repair one emergency at a time. On the nineteenth of April, she suffered a stroke. At that point, her body was going into vasospasms that they had to medicate because the brain, in recognizing an injury, was trying to close off blood vessels to the affected part. But that would mean a lack of oxygen to the brain, which would kill her.

Sam had an angiogram every day, and every day I had to sign off on it. They were simply trying to keep her alive. On the twentieth, only four days later, which felt like a lifetime, they came into her room every hour to administer cognitive tests and assess her responses. They slammed a pencil into her fingernails, hoping for pain.

Nothing.

The right side of her head was so swollen that her eye was shut. That day, they did a tracheotomy and intubated her because she could no longer breathe on her own.

On April 24, we talked to the doctor about Sam's prognosis. He told us it was complicated. The brain is unique, and its recovery process is complex. He told us she would never be the same. Most of the right side of her brain was extensively damaged. The left side of her body was not working, and the stroke had added to the difficulty.

But I began to have hope. We were talking about recovery! She was going to survive! I had no idea Sam would be in the hospital another sixty-eight days.

Perspective Shift

This chapter marks the moment when everything else fades away.

Business, resentment, betrayal, therapy, ambition — all of it vanished when Sam collapsed on the restaurant's bathroom floor. In that instant, there was no "he said, she said." No Seattle. No past. Only this: my wife was dying, and I couldn't breathe.

When she looked up at me from the floor and asked, "Who are you?" — it ripped the last threads of everything I thought I could control. It wasn't anger anymore. It wasn't confusion. It was raw, blinding fear.

And yet, that moment revealed something real and unshakable:

I still loved her.

I still wanted to fight for her.

There was no room for ego. No space for grudges. There was only urgency, survival, and one prayer: Please don't take her from us.

For thirteen days, I didn't leave the hospital. I watched machines breathe for her, surgeries cut her open, and her beautiful face swell beyond recognition — and still, I stayed. Why? Because love doesn't leave when it gets hard. It shows up harder.

This wasn't the story of a perfect marriage. It was the story of imperfect people trying to hold onto love through the unimaginable.

I saw Sam not as the woman who betrayed me, but as the woman I loved...

Who made me laugh in grocery store aisles...

Who let me cry against her when we lost Steve...

Who once said yes to marrying me, even when I had nothing to offer.

Watching her fight for life was the single most painful and transformative thing I've ever experienced. I had nothing left to give but love. And somehow, that was everything.

This chapter isn't about trauma. It's about clarity. It's about realizing what actually matters. When you strip away every layer of bullshit, love is what's left.

And it's enough to build everything on.

—**Trapper**

CHAPTER 16

The Hospital

Jaiden's tenth birthday was April 25. All the plans we'd made had vanished. Seth and Stacey stepped in, gathered her friends, and took them out for the day. I stayed at the hospital. Through the weeks, Jaiden kept to her school schedule, and I made sure to get her there and back. However, she also spent a lot of time at the hospital with me. She would cry or I would cry, and sometimes we'd just collapse into each other. I didn't keep anything from her, and sometimes she was stronger than I was. She was part of almost every doctor/patient conversation because I refused to hide anything from her. We had no idea if Sam would live or die, and I never wanted Jaiden to have to come to me one day and say, "You told me everything was okay!"

We could hope, but we had no guarantees.

Sam was still having constant vasospasms, making any serious medical procedures impossible to perform. The doctors estimated the vasospasms would likely disappear in two weeks. Sam had them for twenty-six days. The doctors were finally able to give her a tracheostomy, and we were sitting in the surgery waiting room when we heard a code blue: Sam had gone into cardiac arrest!

Could it possibly get any worse? Could my emotions bear any more?

They had to.

Sam came out of it and continued to have angiograms almost daily to treat the ongoing vasospasms. Then the doctors discovered another brain bleed, and sepsis - a full-body infection.

Why? What was causing all this? Why Sam? The doctors told us that physical stress was likely the cause of Sam's initial injury. Sam loved working out. I often thought she was the fittest human being alive. The Saturday morning before her injury, she had been at the gym and texted me, "I just felt a pop in my head."

"Do you need to go to the doctor?" I texted back.

"I was working out - I'm okay."

She'd been doing a goblet, a full-body exercise that involves holding a weight in front of your chest and performing a squat. It seemed she was holding her breath, and the strain of moving the weights triggered the aneurysm. At the same time, a blood clot was moving through her brain, and when she pushed, that part of her vein narrowed - between that and the aneurysm, the pressure created an explosion and the subsequent brain bleed.

By late May, she was beginning to make some progress to the point where the physical therapists had her standing beside her bed. I allowed myself to genuinely hope. Surely we had reached an important turning point.

In early June, the doctors found another brain bleed, this one in her cerebellum, a part of her brain that had had no previous issues. I went from high hopes into the deep depths. This was it: my life - one step forward, get kicked in the nuts, and fall ten steps back. One day, I was having conversations with doctors who were telling me how optimistic they were, and the next day, she was on the verge of dying.

They couldn't treat the new bleed without incurring great risk. The only hope we had was that her body would handle the new emergency.

On June 6, Sam was improving again. She was able to follow certain commands with her hands. On June 7, her external ventricular drain (EVD), which drains cerebrospinal fluid from the brain, stopped working. Again, she was barely hanging onto life.

On June 11, she was feeling better again, and one of the nurses pushed her outside in a wheelchair so she could feel the sun on her face and even pluck a red rose from the garden. On June 15, one of her physicians, Dr. Beckman, gave me more news. "We have to put her skull back or she's going to die."

He explained that the skull does more than protect the brain from hard impacts. It also protects it from atmospheric pressure. Without a skull, that pressure could eventually crush the brain. Sam had had a significant part of her skull removed, and it was beginning to affect her cognitive abilities. The problem was that her brain was still swollen, and the pressure of the skull could cause more brain damage.

I asked Dr. Beckman, "If this were your wife, what would you do?"

He said, "I'd put it back on. It's her best chance of having a productive life."

"Let's do it," I said. They reattached her skull and put an internal shunt in her head to drain the cerebrospinal fluid.

On June 21, they inserted a speaking valve because her vocal cord muscles had atrophied. Her first words, very faint, were, "I love you."

It was almost too much to bear. Sam was coming back. I dared to hope again.

A few days later, we got the news that she would be transported to the Craig Hospital, a neurorehabilitation center in Denver. By the end of June, she could swallow and eat soft food. My hope grew from a small candle flicker to a full-fledged bonfire. I remember the day Jaiden and I went to see the Colorado Avalanche win the Stanley Cup, and coming back to the hospital to celebrate the win with Sam and all the nurses.

On June 28, Sam was admitted to Craig Hospital. She was officially no longer a medical risk. My relief was crazy. Those had been the longest seventy-six days I'd ever lived. When she was first admitted, I'd said to Jennifer, my administrative employee, and Brad, a good friend and sales manager, "I'm not going to be working for a while. You guys are just going to have to figure it out." They did an amazing job while I was away.

I didn't work a single day that Sam was in the ICU. Brad and Jenny ran The Garage Doctor for six months. I don't know what would have happened if they had not stepped in and stepped up.

At Craig, Sam was working on her recovery every day, doing speech therapy and every possible kind of physical rehab. In time, the therapists began training Jaiden and me to care for Sam. We learned to do bed transfers, how to take her to the bathroom, and how to look after her personal hygiene needs. By the end of July, she could eat regular food, and in late August, they fitted her into an exoskeleton to help her walk, believing that one day she would regain her mobility.

August 27 was the first day we were allowed to take her out of the hospital. We brought her to Early Bird, our favorite breakfast place, where she was also able to see some of her friends. The outing had a sense of normalcy I hadn't experienced in a long time. From then on, Jaiden and I took her out as often as we were allowed. I brought her to some of Jaiden's soccer games, and on our anniversary, we celebrated with dinner out. Sitting beside her, feeling almost normal, I realized I loved her even more. It wasn't the same needy love as before. Since my attempted suicide and then Sam's accident, something had shifted. I loved Sam with all my heart, but I loved myself too, which allowed me to love Sam not as an extension of me, but as the beautiful individual that she was.

My love also swelled because I had a new understanding of the fragility of life and what a gift it was to be able to live fully. Compared to that, nothing else mattered. Some of the things I thought would kill me—like Sam's infidelity—meant nothing. As long as she was alive, we could love and work it out. And even if we couldn't and went our separate ways, it was more important to be alive than to feel anger or regret.

Perspective Shift

This chapter is a testament to endurance, both physical and emotional. It wasn't just Sam lying in that ICU bed — it was our marriage, our hope, our future, barely clinging to life.

Everything in my life narrowed down to survival:

I stopped thinking in days. I lived moment to moment, crisis to crisis. Seventy-six days felt like seventy-six lifetimes. Every time the doctors handed me another form, another consent slip, another possible "this could kill her" scenario, I signed with trembling hands and silent prayers.

There were glimmers—like watching Sam pick a red rose in the garden or hearing her whisper, "I love you," through her new speaking valve—tiny miracles in a sea of terrifying unknowns.

But what shifted inside me was just as profound.

Before all this, I loved Sam desperately — sometimes out of fear or out of pain. I was constantly chasing worthiness, asking, "Am I good enough? Can I be what she needs?"

But as I sat with her, day after day, watching her battle for life, I began to see that my love didn't need validation.

It was enough.

I was enough.

I stopped needing her to prove anything. Her being alive — that was everything. Her breath. Her presence. Her fight.

And in the middle of all the trauma, I found something unexpected: peace.

Peace in being exactly where I needed to be.

Peace in knowing Jaiden was watching what love really looked like.

Peace in realizing that sometimes love doesn't fix everything — but it's enough to carry you through anything.

That's what this chapter is about.

It's about love that doesn't flinch.

It's about resilience that refuses to quit.

If Sam could fight for her life with that much courage, then I could fight for mine, too.

Let's keep going.

—**Trapper**

CHAPTER 17

Aftermath

We're all human beings doing our best every day. Our feelings will change throughout our lives. We fall in and out of love, and how we love changes. When Sam was in the hospital, all I cared about was that she should live.

Nothing else mattered.

I wish I could find a way for people to understand this perspective on life without having to experience major trauma. There is a level of commitment in this kind of love that is often beyond the reach of most. But it's there if we choose to let go of our petty grievances and simply love for love's sake. When all you care about is another person's life, it no longer matters if they left the cap off the toothpaste or lost the remote control. When I get into an argument with Sam or Jaiden now, I step back and ask myself if this really matters.

It rarely does.

Through all this, I went from being one of the most impatient people alive to a place of peace and understanding. When I'm out with Sam and strangers ask what happened to Sam's leg, assuming perhaps she was in an accident, I'll tell them there's nothing wrong with her leg, but she was in the hospital for a hundred and eighty days with a traumatic brain injury. I want to educate people, even if only in passing, because I want them to think about the fragility of life.

We only get one shot at it. In those days, after all that had happened in such a short period of time, I started thinking about the purpose of life - mine, Jaiden's, Sam's, everyone's life. What was it really all about?

Did I want to keep working at my business?

No.

Why not change?

At about that time, my friend Don, who also owned a garage door company, called and told me he was selling his company. Yes - I could do that. Keeping the same company and living in the same place until I retired or died was not the life I wanted to live.

I want to be fully me, to feel life to its fullest, and, if I can, to change the world or at least help as many people as I can. If I can help one person, it changes the world. Our family doesn't hide who we are. We are willing to be vulnerable, and I think that makes others feel safe as well. And that will have a profound effect.

Sam came home at the end of October, and life changed again. As long as she was in the rehab hospital, people were taking care of her and all her needs. Now, it was up to Jaiden and me - mostly me- and it wasn't easy. Sam needed help getting in and out of bed, using the bathroom, cleaning herself, inserting and changing tampons, and wiping herself. We did it all.

I felt the stress almost immediately, not from the physical work, but from the emotional and mental price I paid when I realized I was no longer Sam's husband. I was her caregiver. I hoped one day she would be able to take care of herself, but for now, she was disabled, and I had to fill a different role.

We had a happy surprise on November 4 when our friends got tickets for the Elton John concert at the Ball Arena. It was hard to get in as we maneuvered Sam's wheelchair to our seats, but she knew every word to every Elton John song, and with the whispery voice she now had, she sang along to every one. That's when I told myself with certainty, "She's going to learn how to talk again."

Later that month, we were able to fly to Seattle to spend Thanksgiving with Sam's mom, but coming back, my stress piled up more. I loved Sam, and I'd always found her body thrilling. We used to have great sex, but that was all gone. I felt nothing. Then the fear set in - what if she never improved? Was this going to be the rest of my life? Was that selfish? Probably, but those were honest thoughts that swirled through my head.

I desperately wanted intimacy, but that was impossible. Maybe my life was just going to suck. However, since Sam was home now, our friends thought everything was quickly returning to normal. They didn't know how hard it was or how far from normal a life we lived.

There were times I would have given anything for a simple married life. I had friends who assumed that as Sam continued to improve, we should just be able to be intimate. They had no idea. I dare you to wipe your wife after a trip to the bathroom and then have sex with her. The emotional wall between husband and caregiver was too solid. The struggle of getting back to being physically attracted to her was and still is very real.

Two and a half years later, I still love her, but I haven't yet scaled that wall. I hope one day I will, and we will be able to connect on that level again.

In the early days, when Sam was still in the hospital, I missed talking to a woman. When I expressed that to my friends, they judged me negatively, and some would relate what they thought were similar stories of a relative having an aneurysm and everything working out just fine. They had no idea. Their situation was not mine.

"I know just what you're going through," they would say.

"No! No, you don't have a clue!"

When people say, "I understand what you're going through," I get that they're trying to be sympathetic. My advice? Stop. You never know someone else's thoughts, feelings, or circumstances. Just listen to what they are willing to tell you. That's all. Just listen. Try to understand. They are not like you or your sister or anyone you have ever known.

You may judge me for what I am about to write, and I understand. I was craving intimacy - going on a date, touching, talking, and laughing together. I met a woman at the hospital whose husband was also in the ICU. We talked almost every day in the waiting room and went out a couple of times, filling a huge void in each of our lives.

What I missed most was intimacy. One night, I met a friend for drinks — a young, single woman I'd always gotten along with. She knew what Sam was going through, and we agreed to an arrangement, knowing I loved Sam and would never leave her, and that I would be completely open with my wife. Maybe I was being selfish. How could I be so upset when Sam was talking with another guy, yet choose to have this arrangement? Was it a fair comparison?

I don't know. All I knew was that if I was going to survive this new stage of my life with Sam, I had to have an intimate relationship with a woman for the sake of my own well-being. And still, I wasn't sure if my decision was *right;* I was only following my gut. What I did require of myself was total honesty with Sam.

Having that conversation with her was tough. I was clear it wasn't about her, but I needed this to face the coming weeks and months. I told her she might not be happy about it and might want to leave me in the future.

She didn't give me her blessing but said, "I just don't want to know about it."

It was never a full-blown affair. We'd go out on a date, and I think the best part for me was feeling like part of a couple again. We were at an Avalanche game once, when we ran into a couple of Sam's friends. The expression on their faces changed from surprise to shock to disgust. I introduced my friend because neither of us was ashamed.

"Does Sam know about this?" one of them asked.

"Yes, she does," I said. "Sam knows her."

They still looked stunned, but I think more by my level of honesty than by the actual act of dating this attractive young woman. I think they were wishing they could be that honest with each other.

If they were truly honest with themselves, I'm willing to bet that more than half the people who have been married twenty or more years would admit that they would like to experience other people. This is not about destroying a marriage. I love Sam, I love our marriage, and I love our family, but I want to experience other people.

I don't date other women today. Sam continues to improve, and we can have real conversations now. The intimacy of really talking with the woman I love fills up a lot of my emotional and intimate holes. We have such an important connection. Still, I believe that if a couple were a hundred percent honest with each other, they might want to change things up now and then. Our rules of marriage were created in a different era. To a large extent, we are following laws written by a group of old men thousands of years ago. Why should I live my life by what they laid out? Is it even applicable today?

The world's population is about eight billion, and I'm supposed to love only one person? It doesn't seem quite right to me, but if you bring the subject up in polite company, you'd better be prepared for some serious blowback. And that's okay. No one has to adopt my point of view, but this is my journey, and in the end, each of us walks their own path.

The arrangement Sam and I have works, but I also wish we could return to the way we were before her injury. I loved being intimate with her, but she's a different person now. Some things we once did that were fun are now work. I hope one day it changes. We both want a physical relationship, but I'm not there yet.

I have one friend who completely gets me and how I feel. His wife died recently from cancer, and he was her caregiver for months before she passed. He knows the line between caregiver and lover; he understands the desire for physical intimacy and the inability to cross that line. He and I have experienced what less than one percent of the world's population goes through. Unless you, too, have been in our situation, you cannot judge us. You can say, "I can't imagine what you're going through daily."

What I went through with Sam changed my life in every possible way. Sam is safe now. She's home, but every day is rehab.

Sam can drive now, and that's a gigantic step forward, not just because it helps with all the domesticity of everyday life but also because it gives her more freedom and feels normal. The more we become a normal couple again, the more likely intimacy will return. I do believe it will happen.

But because everything changed, and I changed, we can never return to how we were. I enjoy spending time with others. I've learned to take care of myself and listen to myself. I used to want the same things Sam does. That was the old Trapper. Today, I want to discover the world. I want to hear other people's stories. The key for me is the willingness to be completely honest with Sam - no secrets, no hiding. I love her too much to be anything other than open and honest with her.

Even more importantly, I've learned to be utterly open and honest with myself, because I've learned that loving and respecting myself has to come first. If nothing else, I hope our story makes you appreciate what you have.

Perspective Shift

This chapter marks a seismic shift — not just in circumstance, but in identity. It's about the raw truth of what happens after survival, when the world expects normal to return... but you know it never will.

I was no longer just Sam's husband — I was her caregiver, and no matter how much love still flowed between us, that shift built a wall between intimacy and duty. It's a wall that no one warns you about. A wall that only those who've been caregivers truly understand.

This chapter isn't about blame or even answers. It's about honesty.

Honesty in recognizing that survival doesn't mean restoration.

Honesty in admitting that I was craving connection, touch, laughter — not to replace my love for Sam, but to survive.

Honesty in sharing the grief of loving someone whose body remains, but whose capabilities — and maybe even personality — have changed.

For so long, I believed love meant sacrifice. But here, I began to understand that love also means truth, even if it's uncomfortable. I told Sam everything — not because I needed permission, but because I respected her enough to be real. And even if it hurt, it was still love. Real love doesn't hide.

In this new life, I wasn't willing to live behind old expectations written for a different generation. I had to ask: What do I need now, as a man, as a father, as a human being who has faced death, betrayal, heartbreak, and rebirth?

This chapter is a declaration:

That we are more than our vows, our mistakes, our roles.

That grief and healing can live in the same house.

That honesty, not perfection, is the foundation of connection.

I'm still walking the line between husband and caregiver, between the life we had and the life we have now. But I walk it with truth, grace, and a hell of a lot more compassion than I used to.

And if I can offer anyone reading this one gift, it's this:

You don't have to break to rebuild. But if you do break — you get to choose what kind of person survives, and rises from the pieces.

—Trapper

Epilogue

In December 2024, I sold The Garage Doctor to a large corporation and fully exited the business by the end of February 2025. My original plan was to work for the company, and I lasted seven days. That was all the evidence I needed to know I am a true entrepreneur. I didn't fit the employee mold.

I wanted to create something new. I also recognized my purpose as helping others live their most fulfilled and successful lives, according to their own definitions of success.

This is what I am passionate about, and the path I am following. I want to inspire others and help them achieve success in their lives, with the understanding that success takes different forms for everyone.

For me, success means living a fulfilled life, and that's about enjoying every day, rather than just making it through. I am focusing on life energy coaching and am well on my way to achieving my goals in that arena. I'm also building an online coaching program to help people understand how they want to live authentically, instead of fitting themselves into a slot society has designed for them.

At age forty-two, I am blessed to understand what success means to me. After everything I've been through—starting life with nothing, finding the love of my life, and almost losing her—my perspective is probably unique. I no longer take my life for granted, and I also no longer invest so much time in the details.

I believe success means different things at different stages of our lives. Today, I feel fulfilled if I am serving others and making a positive difference. Many young people focus on financial success, and that's important. Most of us want a comfortable home, reliable transportation, and a rewarding job—but do you really need an extravagant lifestyle? Ego-driven or society-centric success is not really success at all. We have to know what's important.

I think we need to appreciate what's in our walls—that's what is essential. Sadly, we often don't realize how important those non-tangible items are until we lose them.

I believe success also means living in the moment, and appreciating what I have. If I were to look at my checking account right now and discover a zero balance, it would not affect how I feel in this moment. My success today does not rest on my bank balance. Its foundation is love and caring for others. If I honor myself each day and honor those I love, I am successful and fulfilled.

This feeling is not a static state, but if you're aware of what brings you joy and what fills your heart, you can course correct and return to your state of success.

My daughter often comes to me with problems simply because she's young, and the truly insignificant things matter to her. I'm doing my best to teach her about what really matters. As she grows up, I hope she develops a perspective that allows her to see the big picture so she can focus on what really matters: love, joy, community, family, and developing her own beautiful character.

I'm sure I experienced moments of fulfillment when I was a child, a teenager, and a young adult, but they probably passed unacknowledged. I didn't understand what this "good" feeling was or what had caused it. I wish I'd been aware of what those moments meant back then. I also had to grow into an expanded heart that could truly feel empathy for others and myself. If I had known then what I know now, my life would have been different. However, I am grateful I have this perspective now.

Far too many people reach the end of their lives without ever experiencing genuine fulfillment—and that's sad. I want to do what I can to change that. I want to help other people find their own success and fulfillment.

We all set goals, and that's great. But reaching the goal is not success—success is in the journey. It's okay if you don't attain what you're reaching for. You're successful as long as you move forward on your path every day.

I believe it's great to be goal-oriented, but also, never lose track of what's getting you closer to it: it's you, moving forward, accomplishing mini-goals along the way, and feeling motivated and inspired. Your motivation will inspire others. If you're focused only on the end, you won't be in the present, and you won't feel fulfilled every day. If the end goal is your only focus, your disappointment could be catastrophic if you don't attain it. If you remember to be present for the gifts every day brings, you'll bounce back quickly so you can try again or set a new goal.

Don't sacrifice the people you love for financial gain. Don't give up anything you love or that brings you joy for a goal. Those things you're willing to give up may not seem important now, but you often don't understand how meaningful they are until you no longer have them.

Recognize what's important to you, and always honor yourself.

I came from nothing. Today I have everything. But what is everything? For me, it's living life from my unique perspective and feeling personally fulfilled. *Everything* is feeling good and right inside your skin. *Everything* is waking up in the morning and wanting to explode into the day. I know who I am. Knowing who you are - that's everything.

I went from lost to found.

As we go through life, our behaviors are usually guided by society and our environment, but when you know who you are, you become your own guide. You choose what is right for you - that's everything. That's real freedom.

If you want to find yourself, a good start is asking intentional questions about who you are, and you have to do it often. As we go through life, our focus changes. Ten years ago, I was determined to create an affluent lifestyle where I owned a lot of "stuff." If you ask me about that today, I'll tell you that simplicity brings peace. I believe it was a rapper who said, "Mo' money, mo' problems."

Truth.

If you want success, identify what it is for you. Yours isn't someone else's. But look beyond fast cars and big houses. Ask yourself what makes you excited, what makes your heart sing, and what you love doing so much that you lose track of time. The answers to those questions will lead you to your definition of success.

When I was younger, I focused far too much on financial success and forgot to enjoy the moment.

Today, I'm looking at a wide-open future, and that's exciting. Of course, I'm anxious, but I'm also delighted to have time to choose my path. I know that I want to serve and help as many people as possible. I want to influence them to live a fulfilled life. I want to inspire them through my family's story of trauma, and I want to convince them to make different decisions than some that I made. A few of the things we endured are not so much inspirational as a cautionary tale.

My family went through a lot of pain. If our story can help even one person, perhaps it will have been worthwhile.

We live in a crazy world that seems to have lost sight of the importance of human connection and empathy for others. The world doesn't have to be like that. We've chosen it, and we have the power to choose differently. It's easy to feel helpless in the face of great power. What can one individual do out there? Is our frustration or anger making a difference? Let go of that emotion. Decisions are being made. You have no control over those. Some are made at high government levels, and some may even be decisions you have made. It's over. It's done. Move on, doing the best you can. You decided to get a divorce? Move on. Let go of being a victim. Why get bogged down in recriminations? Let it go and move forward on your path.

I would suggest that you focus on the present. Some people thrive on creating problems. Don't be one of those people. Create joy instead. That's where success and fulfillment lie.

I've learned so many lessons I wish I'd been taught when I was younger. I wish I'd known that when someone attacks you, it generally has nothing to do with you—it's all about the other person's insecurities or issues. I wish I had known that my problems weren't caused by the car I was driving or the house where I lived. I know now that my happiness is all about who I am and living authentically.

We are programmed by society and social media to believe happiness comes from having possessions and a lot of money. Wealthy people know it's not true, but they'll continue to preach it because it will make them even wealthier.

It's time we programmed ourselves to be happy.

If we're not happy with who we are, we can change that. Who you are is a genuine, kind, loving, authentic, and beautiful human being. All you have to do is strip away those things that aren't you. Get rid of that image or persona you've carefully built and nurtured. Be willing to be vulnerable.

Just be you.

This book began as a memoir.

But it was never meant to stop there. My intention wasn't just to tell you what happened to me—it was to show you what's possible for *you*.

Because this isn't about becoming *me*. It's about becoming *you*, fully and unapologetically.

The you that's been buried under pain, pressure, expectations, and fear.

The you that's still in there - waiting to rise.

So here's your next chapter:

Start asking better questions.

Start building new habits.

Start talking to yourself like someone worth saving.

Because you are.

And if no one's told you lately—

Your story isn't over.

Your voice still matters.

And no matter how dark it gets...
light is always an option.

This is where my book ends.

But maybe—just maybe—
this is where your life really begins.

And don't put this book away—not yet. If you're ready to start living your best life, and if you want to understand what your definition of success and fulfillment is, visit me at my website: WWW.TRAPPERSEARLES.COM or scan the QR code on this page.

Let's Go!

— **Trapper**

Acknowledgments

I put a good deal of thought into who to acknowledge at the end of this book. Who has made a difference in my life? Who has influenced me and been there for me when I needed them? Who has been my friend through all the ups and downs?

I've been blessed with having a long list of special people. I only hope that I don't leave anyone out. If I do, please forgive me and know that I thank you.

My parents, Tom and Shellie Searles: Thank you for doing your best with the limited resources available. I always admired your grit and am grateful you passed that on to me.

My father-in-law, Steve Muscatel: I learned so much from you and what you valued. You included people in your life and always made them feel comfortable. When someone needed help, you were there for them. You made me feel seen, and you recognized my authentic spirit. Thank you.

My mother-in-law, Debbie Muscatel: Our relationship has evolved and deepened with the years. You have always been open with me, supportive, and encouraging, and you have consistently made me feel part of your family. I love you.

Amber and Trevor Hayes, my sister and brother-in-law: You always picked me up when I was down and helped me through so many tough times. Thank you.

JD and Maryanne Henley: Thank you for taking me in as part of the family and treating me like a normal kid. You always made sure that I felt like I mattered.

Sally Oates, my high school gym teacher: You always gave me a safe place when I was having such a hard time as an insecure high schooler.

The Fowler family: Thank you for providing a place that felt normal in the midst of chaos. And a special thank you to Jared Fowler for being more like a brother than a friend for most of my life. I wish we were closer; I love you, buddy.

Seth Henley: Thank you for being my best friend since I was twelve and supporting me through so many challenges. I wouldn't be where I am today without your support and friendship. I love you, man.

Stacey Henley: I appreciate you being a great friend and helping me survive that hard time when Sam was so ill. I couldn't have done it without your support. I love you.

Josh and Amanda Wadsworth: Josh, you've been a great friend since Little League, and you're still a great, wonderful, supportive friend. I look forward to our continued friendship. Love you, man. Amanda and the boys, I love you all so much!

Brian and Jessica Sorrenson: Thank you for being solid, dependable friends through some of my life's most challenging times, and for being so supportive of my business and of me as an entrepreneur. I love you both.

Roy and Ron Parmely: I'm so fortunate to have worked for you when I was young. I learned more than you know, which helped me create a great life.

Jim Bauman: When I first moved to Colorado, you helped keep me in line. Thank you.

Nate Vielehr: Thank you for welcoming me into Sam's group of friends and making me feel like I belonged. You've been a great friend for such a long time. I love you.

Chase Larson: I'm so thankful for what our friendship has become. You've become my "Go To" for anything and I always know you'll be there. I love you, man. You're the best..

Brad and Julie Styve: You have always been supportive of me and my family, and you've always treated us like family. I love you both. Thank you.

Josh Elliot: Thank you for being a great friend since Little League. I'm just super happy that our friendship has grown stronger with time.

Walt Dublin: Fitness connected us; trauma bonded us. You're one of my best friends, and I love you.

Ryan Blair: I'm so grateful that our paths crossed, when I needed acknowledgement and validation with this book; you were there to guide me and provide opportunities I otherwise wouldn't have seen.

My daughter, Jaiden: What can I possibly say to you or about you? You saved my life, Stinkybean, and I love you forever.

Sam: You're a real pain in the ass, but you will always be my sweet potato. For some reason, I will never stop loving you. We have been through so much together and it has created a great strength in our relationship.

Lastly, I want to thank Authors on Mission who have helped me write this book and bring it to life. Special thanks to Goody Lindley, my editor and writing mentor. Without her, I would not have been able to do this. My deepest gratitude.

About the Author

**Trapper Searles is a builder—of ideas,
of people, and of perspective.**

A lifelong entrepreneur and leader, he launched his first company, The Garage Doctor, at just 21 and spent nearly two decades growing it into Denver's most trusted names in home services. But Trapper's true transformation began when life hit harder than any business challenge ever could.

After surviving a turbulent childhood, enduring personal breakdowns, and becoming a full-time caregiver to his wife following a traumatic brain injury, he emerged with something far more valuable than success: *clarity*.

Today, Trapper is a perspective expert, energy lifecoach, and author of *I Survived Suicide by Killing Myself*—a raw, powerful look at what it takes to rise from the ashes of your own identity. His mission is simple but bold: to help others rebuild their lives from the inside out, with authenticity, energy, and purpose.

When he's not speaking or coaching, you'll find him outdoors, at the gym, or enjoying time with his wife and daughter—the real reasons behind everything he builds.

www.ingramcontent.com/pod-product-compliance
Lightning Source LLC
Chambersburg PA
CBHW031418120626
46545CB00006B/2166